WITHDRAWN
UTSA Libraries

THE ANATOMY OF MEDIATION

What Makes It Work

THE ANATOMY OF MEDIATION

What Makes It Work

Sam Kagel
Kathy Kelly

The Bureau of National Affairs, Inc., Washington, D.C.

Copyright © 1989
The Bureau of National Affairs, Inc.

Second Printing April 1992

Library of Congress Cataloging-in-Publication Data

Kagel, Sam.
  The anatomy of mediation.

  Includes index.
  1. Mediation and conciliation, Industrial—United States.   2. Mediation and conciliation, Industrial.   3. Mediation.   I. Kelly, Kathy, 1951–   II. Title.
  HD5504.A3K28 1989   302.3   88-34086
  ISBN 0-87179-599-X

Authorization to photocopy items for internal or personal use, or the internal or personal use of specific clients, is granted by BNA Books for libraries and other uses registered with the Copyright Clearance Center (CCC) Transactional Reporting Service, provided that $0.50 per page is paid directly to CCC, 27 Congress St., Salem, MA 01970, 0-87179-599-X/89/$0 + .50.

Printed in the United States of America
International Standard Book Number 0-87179-599-X

Preface

Much is being written these days about why courts do not work. We have chosen to write about something that can work. Mediation can generate constructive solutions for many problems with less cost and less hostility than any alternative.

Before you accept this conclusion, we expect that you will want to know what makes mediation work effectively. That is the purpose of this book. We seek to describe what makes mediation work and why it can be useful to people involved with business disputes, family problems, employment matters, and a host of other controversies.

The text is designed to take the mystery out of the mediation process. If you face disputes of the kind noted, we hope the book will answer any questions or doubts you have about the possible usefulness of mediation. If you work in the mediation field, you will find detailed guidance in the text about techniques necessary for successful mediation.

We thank all of our colleagues whose ideas and encouragement have contributed to this effort. We also thank all those who have provided us with the past mediation experiences generating the ideas reflected here.

Sam Kagel
San Francisco, California
January 1989

Kathy Kelly
Professor of Law
McGeorge School of Law
Sacramento, California

Introduction

Francis Bacon wrote, "It is generally better to deal by speech than by letter; and by the mediation of a third than by a man's self."[1] Some cultures, notably that of China, have persistently agreed with Bacon in his conclusion that mediation is the best way to solve problems.[2] Until recently, however, public and private institutions in the United States have not promoted mediation. Our tax dollars have gone to pay for courts in which attorneys argue and judges or juries make decisions about our disputes. The resources spent to support mediation have been minuscule by comparison.

Some would say this has happened because many state legislators, who draft laws, are lawyers and they have striven to create more income for their own kind. The American preference for litigation over mediation does have some more "pure" causes, however. Our country's founders stressed the rights of individuals, and our culture teaches that individual rights are to be honored, respected, and protected. Reliance on courts for dispute resolution is consistent with this value. Courts provide every individual with an opportunity to hear his cause argued with the greatest vigor. We have looked to courts as the means to protect our individual liberties, and they have flourished in that role.

In recent years, however, an increasing number of people have adopted the view that courts and lawyers are not the protectors of our liberties, but rather the captors. One system, litigation, seems to have too great a lock on a vast majority of problems. Many individuals and businesses are asking, "Can't many problems be solved without the accusations, complications, and expense that court cases entail?" Lawyers and others alike are looking for answers to that question, and mediation is one of the principal places they are looking.

Mediation is an effort by a person or group of persons who have

---

[1] THE ESSAYS OF FRANCIS BACON, XLVII OF NEGOTIATING (M.A. Scott, 1908).
[2] Cohen, *Chinese Mediation on the Eve of Modernization*, 54 CALIF. L. REV. 1209 (1966).

no direct stake in a problem to bring those directly interested to the point of agreement about how the problem should be resolved. Unlike a courtroom judge, a mediator has no authority to impose any particular outcome. The persons directly affected must agree on a result, and if they do not, they are left in the same position they were in before attempting settlement. A detailed comparison of mediation to other processes for resolving conflict (such as negotiation, arbitration, litigation, med-arb, and mini-trials) is contained in Chapter 4.

In the last ten years, this country has experienced a mediation boom that rivals the postwar baby boom. Historically, mediation in America has enjoyed its greatest use and support in labor disputes. In 1947, Congress created the Federal Mediation and Conciliation Service, which provides mediators to minimize the chances of strikes resulting from deadlocked talks over labor contracts. Use of these mediators has long been mandatory in some industries. Disputants in these and other industries have also used private mediators for many years.

This old idea is now being advanced as the new solution to endless sorts of problems other than labor disputes. In 1983, mediation was used to solve a long-standing dispute over a proposed flood-control dam in the state of Washington. By mid-1984, mediators across the country had been brought in to assist with over 160 environmental disputes.[3] In 1980, California passed legislation requiring mediation of child custody and visitation disputes.[4] Success and satisfaction with this program in California have caused other states to follow suit.[5] Mediation has been suggested as the best means to eliminate racial violence,[6] handle nonfelony crimes,[7] and address a host of other problems.

Although the mediation bandwagon is rolling, some resist getting on board. Despite new uses of mediation, far less is known about this process in our society than is known about court proceedings. There have not been any long-running TV shows portraying mediation as the route to justice or reconciliation. Many people have the following questions about mediation:

---

[3]Bingham, *Resolving Environmental Disputes: A Decade of Experience*, 17 RESOLVE 1 (1986).
[4]CAL. CIV. CODE §4607 (Deering, 1984).
[5]See L. Freedman, LEGISLATION ON DISPUTE RESOLUTION (ABA Special Committee on Dispute Resolution, Monograph Series No. 2, 1982).
[6]Dibrell, *Mediation in Civil Rights Issues—The Port Arthur Experience*, THE POLICE CHIEF, November 1976, p. 80.
[7]Rice, *Mediation and Arbitration as a Civil Alternative to the Criminal Justice System—An Overview and Legal Analysis*, 29 AM. U. L. REV. 17 (1979).

"I don't want to be pressured to 'split the baby'—isn't that what would happen in mediation?"

"I've tried to settle, but the other side is hopeless—what can a mediator accomplish?"

"I don't want to spend time educating an outsider about my problems when there's no certainty anything will come of it—shouldn't I be in court where I know an outcome will be declared one way or the other?"

These are very logical and important questions. Simple definitions of mediation do not clarify what it can accomplish or why it works. The mediation process has existed throughout human history, and it has not changed significantly during that time. Barton gave the following description of a "monkalun" or "go-between" who played an established mediator's role in a primitive society:

> The office of the *monkalun* is the most important one to be found in Ifugao society. The *monkalun* is a whole court, completely equipped, in embryo. He is judge, prosecuting and defending counsel, and the court record. His duty and his interest are for a peaceful settlement . . . . To the end of peaceful settlement he exhausts every art of Ifugao diplomacy. He wheedles, coaxes, flatters, threatens, drives, scolds, insinuates . . . . The *monkalun* has no authority. All he can do is to act as a peace making go-between. His only power is in his art of persuasion, his tact and his skillful playing on human emotions and motives.[8]

Mediators still wheedle, coax, flatter, threaten, drive, scold, and insinuate. They also continue to have "no authority." It is natural to question what a process such as this, with no certainty of reaching any definitive conclusion, has to offer. Yet, William Simkin, one of this country's most noted labor mediators, has offered the opinion that, "the power of persuasion can be more potent than the powers of compulsion or suppression."[9]

What leads Simkin to prefer mediation, the power to persuade, over the power to order? What makes mediation successful? How can it accomplish anything where best efforts at negotiation have failed? Should the mediation bandwagon continue to roll, and if so, in what direction? Should lawyers and others consider mediation a prime option for resolving disputes? Asking and answering these questions is the purpose of this book.

---

[8] R. Barton, IFUGAO LAW 87 (1969), discussed in Fuller, *Mediation—Its Forms and Functions*, 44 S. CAL. L. REV. 305, 338 (1971).
[9] W. Simkin, MEDIATION AND THE DYNAMICS OF COLLECTIVE BARGAINING (BNA Books, 1971), p. 357. A second edition of this work, co-authored with Nicholas A. Fidandis, was published by BNA Books in 1986.

These questions are not answered in essay fashion. They are answered by presenting the experience of the authors as to what produces success in mediation, principally through a realistic Case Study that allows the reader to observe a complete mediation.

The Case Study

Most of what a mediator does is part of two simply stated tasks: (1) helping to define problems, and (2) aiding in the solution of problems. The things a successful mediator does to accomplish these tasks may, and will be, listed; this recitation alone does not really convey very much about successful mediation. The most difficult challenge in mediation is the determination of timing. A given strategy may cause failure at one time, but may bring success at another.

For this reason, the Case Study that follows this Introduction has been made the central part of this book. It is written as the script for a play would be, so that the reader may see every move the Mediator makes. Thus, the timing decisions of the Mediator are revealed. When should the parties be brought together, and when should they be kept apart? When should the Mediator listen patiently, and when should ideas or observations be put forth? Is it time for around-the-clock talks or time for a hiatus to let tempers cool? The strategy of making these decisions is best conveyed through example, and that is the purpose of the Case Study.

The topic of the Case Study is a labor-management dispute. An Opera in a large city has had a collective bargaining agreement with the Musicians Union for some time. As the expiration date for the current agreement nears, the parties find themselves unable to agree on a new contract; they remain far apart on several significant issues. Both parties seek mediation 13 days before a strike deadline. They decide to select a private mediator, rather than using one supplied by a government agency.

Many of the issues raised in this Case Study are drawn from mediation experiences of the authors. While the developments in the Study are realistic, they are not intended to portray actual developments in any particular mediation. Likewise, the characters in the Study are not intended to portray any actual persons.

The choice of a labor problem for the Study is not accidental. Everyone is familiar with the sorts of issues that arise in labor negotiations. And, as will be explained more fully in Chapters 2 and 3, the techniques displayed here may be used successfully in mediation of commercial, environmental, and family disputes, as well as all other problems arising from human relationships. Chapter 4, which defines other processes for resolving conflict, also highlights the comparative benefits mediation can afford, when pursued through the techniques presented in this book.

The techniques displayed in this book should have utility not only for professional mediators, but also for others. If you are a businessperson who encounters disputes, this text will illustrate how mediation can lead to good solutions which do not simply "split the baby." It will also display why mediation can produce settlement even though negotiations have stalled.

If you are a lawyer, you will find reason to conclude that your participation in mediation may accomplish better protection of your client's interests than participation in a trial can offer. You will also find guidance regarding the elements necessary for successful mediation.

The text has another valuable use which should not be overlooked. Nearly everyone could become a better negotiator by employing the techniques necessary for successful mediation. As will be seen, use of these techniques frequently leads to a better understanding of everyone's vital interests, thereby enabling solutions that do not exact painful concessions. Since we all must negotiate with others over differences as part of our work or personal lives, these skills have clear value to us all.

Contents

Preface v

Introduction vii

Chapter 1. A Case Study: Effective Mediation in Action 1
Day Number 1 3
  Joint Session 1:30 P.M. 9
  Summary of Events 16
  Private Conversation 5:00 P.M. 17
Day Number 3 21
  Meeting with Employer Representative 9:45 A.M. 21
  Joint Session 10:00 A.M. 22
  Private Conversation 11:00 A.M. 23
  Further Private Conversation 3:00 P.M. 27
  Meeting with Union Committee 3:30 P.M. 27
  Meeting with Employer Committee 4:30 P.M. 31
  Meeting with Union Committee 5:00 P.M. 37
  Meeting with Employer Committee 5:30 P.M. 42
  Meeting with Union Committee 6:00 P.M. 45
  Meeting with Employer Committee 6:15 P.M. 47
  Memorandum of Pension Settlement 48
  Meeting with Employer Committee 7:00 P.M. 49
  Summary of Events 53
  Private Conversation 7:30 P.M. 54
  Joint Session 8:30 P.M. 61
  Joint Session 10:30 P.M. 64
  Summary of Events 66
  Private Conversation 11:30 P.M. 67
Day Number 4 68
  Joint Session 10:00 A.M. 68
  Private Conversation 12:30 P.M. 70
  Conversation with Union Committee 3:40 P.M. 74
  Summary of Events 74

Private Conversation 4:30 P.M. 75
Day Number 6 76
  Joint Session 1:30 A.M. 81
  Summary of Events 82
  Private Conversation 2:00 A.M. 83
Day Number 7 84
  Private Conversation 3:30 P.M. 84
Days Number 8 and 9 86
  Joint Session Number 1 86
  Joint Session Number 2 89
  Summary of Events 93
  Private Conversation Following Settlement of These Issues 94
Day Number 10 95
  Meeting with Employer Committee 11:00 A.M. 95
  Meeting with Union Committee 5:30 P.M. 99
  Meeting with Union Committee 7:30 P.M. 101
  Meeting with Employer Committee 7:45 P.M. 102
  Joint Session 8:00 P.M. 103
  Summary of Events 104
  Private Conversation Late on Day 10 105

Chapter 2. Dissecting the Case Study: What Were the Keys to Success? 109

A. *Improving Effectiveness—Setting the Stage for Success* ... 109
  WHO? 110
    1. Are All "Parties" Present at the Mediation Sessions? ... 110
    2. Working with a Manageable Number of Participants 112
    3. Getting to Know the "Cast of Characters" 113
  WHAT? 114
    4. Joint Meetings versus "Shuttle Diplomacy" 114
  WHY? 116
    5. Realistic Optimism—The Mediator Is Not a Magician .. 116
    6. The Role of Patience—"You Cannot Eat a Hot Bun in One Bite" 117
    7. Obtaining the Trust of the Parties 118
  WHERE? 119
    8. The Location of Meetings 119
  WHEN? 120
    9. The Order of Attack 120
B. *Identifying the Conflicts* 123
    10. What Are the Issues as the Parties See Them? 123

11. Peeling the Artichoke—Finding the Heart of the Matter	123
12. Pressing for Known Facts and Discovering Unknown Facts	125
C. *Resolving the Conflicts*	129
13. Bringing the Facts to Bear	129
14. Converting "Agreements in Theory" to Agreements in Fact and Firming Up Tentative Agreements	131
15. Creativity—How Does the Mediator Promote New Ideas?	132
16. Horsetrading—Finding Agreeable Exchanges	135
17. What Are Each Party's Pressure Points?	136
18. Discovering Each Party's "Secret Heart"	138
19. The Mediator as a "Third Negotiator—Neutral, but Not Neutered"	139
20. When to Talk and When Not to Talk	151
21. Timing—How Are These All-Important Decisions Made?	152
22. Alternatives to Mediation—Do They Play a Role?	153
D. *Finalizing the Deal*	154
23. Suggesting Wording of Proposals for Clarity and Salability	154
24. Prompt Drafting of the Settlement	155
25. Enforcement of the Settlement	155
E. *Conclusion*	157
Chapter 3. Application to Varied Settings	158
Situation No. 1. A Complex Business Dispute	158
Situation No. 2. A Sex Harassment Claim	163
Situation No. 3. A Neighborhood Problem	172
Situation No. 4. A Custody Dispute	176
Situation No. 5. A Family Problem	181
Chapter 4. Comparing Mediation to the Alternatives	184
Force	184
Negotiation	184
Mediation	185
Arbitration	186
Mediation-Arbitration (Med-Arb)	188
Courts	188
Other Combinations of These Techniques	189

Is Mediation the Best of These? 190

Appendix 193
    Table A. Pension Benefits 193
    Table B. Time and Money Guarantees 196

Index 201

About the Authors 205

Chapter 1
A Case Study: Effective Mediation in Action

As you read the Case Study, you may feel the need for some outline that will help to organize your thoughts about what the Mediator is accomplishing. Everything done by the Mediator in the Study serves one of four central purposes:

A. *Improving* his *effectiveness* as a confidant and persuader;
B. *Identifying* areas of *conflict*;
C. *Resolving* the *conflicts*; and
D. *Finalizing* the *deal*.

Listed below are 25 topics or questions that arise in the course of striving to accomplish these central purposes. They are collected in logical groups here, and they will be discussed in the same order in Chapter 2, which summarizes the mediation skills displayed in the Case Study. Reality, however, is not so well ordered. Since the Case Study portrays a mediation realistically, these topics emerge and re-emerge within it, as the situation warrants.

A. Improving Effectiveness—Setting the Stage for Success

1. Are all "Parties" present at the mediation sessions?
2. Working with a manageable number of participants and "You cannot wrap fire in paper"
3. Getting to know the "cast of characters"
4. Joint meetings Versus "shuttle diplomacy"
5. Realistic optimism—The mediator is not a magician

6. The role of patience—"You cannot eat a hot bun in one bite"
7. Obtaining the trust of the parties
8. The location of meetings
9. The order of attack

B. Identifying the Conflicts

10. What are the issues as the parties see them?
11. Peeling the artichoke—finding the heart of the matter
12. Pressing for known facts and discovering unknown facts

C. Resolving the Conflicts

13. Bringing the facts to bear
14. Converting "agreements in theory" to agreements in fact and firming up tentative agreements
15. Creativity—how does the mediator promote new ideas?
16. Horsetrading—finding agreeable exchanges
17. What are each party's pressure points?
18. Discovering each party's "secret heart"
19. The mediator as a "third negotiator—neutral, but not neutered"
20. When to talk and when not to talk
21. Timing—how are these all-important decisions made?
22. Alternatives to mediation—do they play a role?

D. Finalizing the Deal

23. Suggesting wording of proposals for clarity and salability
24. Prompt drafting of the settlement
25. Enforcement of the settlement

To assist you in tracking these issues, the numbers shown to the left of each item in the list above will be used as reference guides in the margin every time a topic from the list is discussed throughout the remainder of the book. As already indicated, Chapter 2 summarizes what is portrayed about these issues in the Case Study. Chapter 3 displays how the mediation skills demonstrated in the Case Study and detailed in Chapter 2 may be successfully used to address disputes arising in a wide variety of contexts.

In the Appendix of this book, you will also find Tables that summarize the positions taken by the parties on some of the more complex issues during the mediation. These Tables may be of assistance in following the factual developments that unfold.

Day Number 1

MEDIATOR: Well, you wanted an opportunity to observe a mediation and you will have that chance beginning today at 1:30 P.M.

OBSERVER: What's going to happen?

MEDIATOR: Negotiations have been taking place over a period of eight months for a new collective bargaining agreement between the Opera and the Musicians Union. Believe it or not, in that time only *one* issue has been resolved; that relates to funeral leave. Nineteen significant issues still remain to be resolved. The parties have asked me to mediate settlement of those 19 issues.

OBSERVER: Those facts don't give much cause for optimism, do they?

MEDIATOR: I know that both sides want to reach a settlement. If that weren't true, they wouldn't ask me to mediate. But they've clearly been operating at arm's-length and with great caution. It looks like both sides have been unwilling to compromise for fear of getting nothing in return. I'm going to have to make both sides confident that a settlement can and will be reached in order to get some movement.

OBSERVER: Have you learned anything specific about the circumstances or the precise issues?

MEDIATOR: I spoke with a representative of each side when arrangements were made for the mediation. The Union supplied me with a list of the outstanding disputes, but it doesn't disclose much. I know that the parties are up against a deadline. The Opera is scheduled to begin rehearsing for its first series of performances 13 days from today. If a new contract settlement is not reached by that time, the rehearsals will not begin and the first series of performances may have to be canceled.

OBSERVER: Why can't the rehearsals begin anyway?

MEDIATOR: A few years ago, the orchestra held up a performance in order to force one last concession before finalizing a contract settlement. The Opera is unwilling to put itself in a position where that could happen again.

OBSERVER: Isn't that going to make your job more difficult?

MEDIATOR: Well, more often than not, the threat of a strike or lockout is a part of contract negotiations between labor and management. It can be very helpful to have a clear deadline by which work cannot or will not continue if there is no settlement. That encourages both sides to trim the fat from their proposals and get down to the essentials.

OBSERVER: I don't quite understand how the threat of a strike can help you.

MEDIATOR : A mediator, as contrasted with an arbitrator, has no power or authority to impose a final solution. For this reason, a mediator must make the best use of "pressure points" that can aid in bringing about the movement necessary for a settlement. The mediator in a case must identify the "pressure points" very early. Reminding the parties at critical steps of the costs associated with any alternative to settlement can help to inspire movement.

OBSERVER: What are the "pressure points" available to a mediator that may give him or her some muscle to aid in persuading the parties to settle an issue in dispute?

Understand external pressures
<17>

MEDIATOR: In a labor-management case the threat of a strike or lockout is an important "pressure point." In other settings, such as business or family disputes, the threat of a civil suit with the prospect of extended litigation at substantial cost may be used as a "pressure point." No matter how strongly the law seems to favor one party, it can't be sure of winning in court, so the risky nature of that alternative is something I discuss. For example, many people who file lawsuits are "hungry"—they need some money now and can't afford to plod through years of litigation in order to find out if it might be possible to win slightly more. If a proposal looks appropriate, I'll remind a "hungry" plaintiff that it could be a very long time before he or she sees any more. And external pressures such as public opinion may be present in some cases.

OBSERVER: Have you learned anything else about the circumstances or the issues?

Confer with each party before meeting
<18>

MEDIATOR: Well, as I said, I spoke very briefly with a representative of each party when arrangements were made for today's meeting. I understand that the unresolved issues include both money demands and contract language problems. The money demands are going to be very difficult to resolve because, I am told, the Opera has lost money in recent years. The Union representative tells me that the parties have had just as much difficulty dealing with some of the critical contract language issues.

OBSERVER: Is it proper to have private conversations with one party or the other as you describe?

MEDIATOR: It is not only proper, it's absolutely essential. There are 19 issues that the parties have not been able to resolve by talking to each other. In order to make progress now I need to extract some information from each party that they have not been able or willing to share across the table.

OBSERVER: Who exactly is going to be at the meeting this afternoon?

MEDIATOR: Each side has a committee of five people who have participated in the negotiations. Full committees from both sides will be present when we meet.

OBSERVER: Couldn't you get a little more accomplished if you didn't have such a large audience?

MEDIATOR: In the first place, they're not part of an audience; they are *participants*. Mediation is not a show put on by the mediator. It's a continuation of negotiations and negotiation can't produce a settlement unless the participants, in this case both sides' committee members, become willing to make some changes in position. So, their presence is absolutely vital if anything is to be accomplished.

OBSERVER: What do you mean when you say that mediation is a continuation of negotiations?

MEDIATOR: Well, the parties, as I told you, have been negotiating for eight months. They were unable to reach an agreement on all their differences. So I have been called in as a mediator, in effect, to participate in the negotiations. Everyone, including me, will be working to negotiate a solution without a strike.

OBSERVER: I've read of some negotiations in which the committees had 25 or more people. Can you really negotiate with that many people?

Work with a manageable number of people
<2>

MEDIATOR: If the committees are that large, I ask each side to select a subcommittee of three to five people. Sometimes I hold a preliminary meeting with everyone to review the outstanding issues so that I can explain how the mediation will proceed. When actual negotiating begins, however, it's necessary to have a smaller group so that people won't behave like they're on stage.

OBSERVER: You said before that the mediator is a negotiator. Could you explain that a little further?

The mediator's role:

MEDIATOR: In effect, I will be a third party to the negotiations. Negotiators seek to persuade each other as to their respective positions on an issue so that a mutually agreeable solution is reached. I will seek to persuade the parties to enter an area where settlement is possible, and, when necessary, persuade them to adopt a specific agreement on the issue in dispute.

OBSERVER: Would you say that you are a persuader or a facilitator? I've seen both those terms used to describe mediators.

MEDIATOR: My function, on each issue, is to show the parties how to aim at the same pot so they can both hit it without messing on each other. Now you can call that persuading, or facilitating, or both, so far as I'm concerned.

OBSERVER: I'll save my questions about how that's done until I see you in action! You said that you will seek to persuade the parties. Does each committee member usually have an equal say when it comes to making changes in position?

Try to assure decision-makers are present
<1>

MEDIATOR: Generally, Union committee members have an equal say in deciding whether a settlement will be recommended to the full membership. Ratification by the full membership is almost always required. Employer committees are usually organized differently. Some of the members may be there only to provide information; they may have no authority to make decisions. Sometimes the person who is really calling the shots isn't even *in* the negotiations. That's a bad situation because then the real decision-maker doesn't have the benefit of what goes on in the mediation. For that reason, whenever I'm in a position to have some choice, I suggest that the real decision-makers participate directly.

OBSERVER: Have you had experience with someone on the outside of negotiations calling the shots?

MEDIATOR: Yes. I was mediating a Pacific Coast Longshore strike that had been going on for 136 days. I was able to get the parties negotiating toward an agreement on a crucial issue, but then the employer representative told me he would have to check it out with his executive committee. This was at 2:00 A.M. on the sixth day of a very difficult mediation. I blew my stack and said I wanted to meet this committee.

OBSERVER: What happened?

MEDIATOR: I met the committee and told them that I would not mediate with absentee negotiators; that if they wanted to be part of the negotiations, they should come into the arena. As to the particular issue, I gave them two minutes to agree or disagree and told them if they disagreed I was pulling out of the mediation.

OBSERVER: That was a pretty tough stand.

MEDIATOR: Yes. But when the participating negotiators reach an agreement on a specific issue they should not be affected by the veto power of invisible representatives for either party. Those invisible representatives won't know what has led up to a particular proposal. Don't forget, when the *entire* package is agreed upon, it may be subject to ratification by the negotiators' principals. And everyone needs to remember that unless deals are "salable" at that time, they are meaningless. But, when the settlement is examined then, there will be time to appropriately review all of the background that produced it.

OBSERVER: How will you begin this afternoon?

Get to know the cast of characters

<3>

MEDIATOR: As I mentioned before, a settlement can't be produced unless the participants become willing to make some changes in position. In order to promote that, I have to get to know the participants —the cast of characters. The desires and priorities of each committee member are going to be influential, so I have to get acquainted quickly.

OBSERVER: How will you do that?

MEDIATOR: First I will have a joint meeting with all the members of both committees to hear a preliminary summary of the outstanding issues. During this meeting, I will begin to size up the negotiators. Who are the spokespeople? What is the demeanor of each committee? As a result of what I hear and see, I begin to develop the approach I will try to follow.

OBSERVER: Then what will you do?

MEDIATOR: I'll ask to meet with each committee separately. I won't cover each and every issue at that time in detail. I'll just try to get to know the people I'm dealing with. There should be an opportunity for each committee member to give his candid general perspective on the negotiations.

OBSERVER: What does that accomplish?

Identify the priorities of participants
<10>

MEDIATOR: It will help me begin to figure out what is most important to each negotiator. When I listen to each Union committee member, for example, I'll be forming an impression in my mind about that. Is this someone with substantial outside employment who's more interested in contract language than money? Is this a long-time employee whose main concern is benefits for retirees? Or is this a younger member of the orchestra who needs to see more money on the paycheck?

OBSERVER: What else will you do when you meet informally?

MEDIATOR: I'll certainly try to find out if there's anyone in the wings calling shots. As I said before, it can cause problems if there are decision-makers who are not participating. It helps me to find out early whether that's the case so I know who, in addition to those present, needs to be sold on any solution.

Build confidence in your experience and suggestions
<7>

And I'll do a little bit of personal salesmanship designed to create trust in me. Very shortly I'll be making suggestions to both parties, and they need to believe that I know what I'm talking about. So, I'll tell them about some of my past experience, in a low-key way. I'll work in as many stories as I can to make clear that my suggestions are based on knowledge of collective bargaining issues gained through participation in many negotiations and mediations.

OBSERVER: How will you proceed after meeting informally with each of the committees?

MEDIATOR: There's really no way to decide that now. I'll just have to see what develops.

Joint Session 1:30 P.M.
(All Committee Members Present)

Encourage ban on media campaigns

MEDIATOR: We need to begin by setting some guidelines about how we will operate and my role as a mediator. First, let's talk about the media. Your dispute is "hot" news. In my experience, negotiations such as these are never helped if the parties try to carry on a media campaign with the press. I'm sure that you will be contacted by press representatives that need a story, and I'm sympathetic with their position. But, until we reach a settlement, there's too great a danger that only part of the story will be reported, and that will just make the job each of you must do with the people you represent harder. I suggest, so long as these mediations continue, that if either side is approached, you simply indicate that negotiations are in progress and nothing more can be said. Is that acceptable?

EMPLOYER REPRESENTATIVE: Yes.

UNION REPRESENTATIVE: Does that mean you'll follow the same ground rule?

MEDIATOR: Absolutely. I won't issue any statements unless they are jointly approved by the parties.

> Set a positive tone by:
>
> 1. Emphasizing causes for optimism
> <5>

Let me say a few words before we get into specific issues. I understand that there are 19 unresolved issues on the table. As you know, I received a list of the 19 issues that are outstanding, and I have reviewed that list. I have two observations which I would like to pass on to you. First, it's my clear conclusion that an agreement on all of these issues is quite possible. By making that observation, I don't mean to belittle the significance of any of these issues. I know that they would not have remained on the table until this time if they didn't relate to very pressing concerns. But all of the issues, both economic and noneconomic, are similar to questions that I have seen raised and resolved in other mediations. So there is nothing here that can't be dealt with effectively.

> 2. Encouraging flexibility
> <5>
>
> 3. Placing responsibility on the parties (The mediator is not a magician.)
> <5>

Obviously, however, an agreement is not going to be possible unless there is some movement from both sides. You must understand from the beginning that a mediator is not a magician. I can't produce an agreement out of thin air. I'm going to do my best to find out through joint and separate meetings what is in your "secret heart" on each issue. And I'll judge the possibilities for settlement in light of that information.

But, in the final analysis, an agreement only occurs when the parties reach a mutual understanding. For that to happen, both of you are going to have to change your positions in some respect. I hope and expect that you are prepared to do that.

Further Developments: The Mediator very briefly explained alternatives other than strike or lockout such as orthodox arbitration and med-arb (see Chapter 4) to the parties. Both parties should be familiarized with a range of options at the beginning of a mediation because one of these processes may become appropriate for use at a later stage concerning part or all of the dispute. For example, a mediated agreement may be reached on everything except one or two important issues where an impasse exists. The parties may decide that using orthodox arbitration or med-arb for the impasse issues makes more sense than a strike or lockout.

Then the Mediator invited the parties to briefly explain their respective positions regarding each of the outstanding 19 issues. He assured that each side was able to summarize its views on the issues without interruptions from the other party. After this was done, the following took place:

> MEDIATOR: Now I'd like to meet with each committee separately for a short while before I make any suggestions about how we should proceed. There's a back conference room and a front office, so make yourselves comfortable.

Further Developments: The Mediator met with the Union committee first and then the Employer committee. He learned that some members of the Union committee were experienced musicians with lengthy service and various sources of outside income. These members naturally expressed more interest in retirement benefits. There were also younger members of the committee who gave highest priority to work guarantees and wages. It was clear, however, that the two groups were committed to support one another.

As he left to meet with the Employer group, the Mediator told the Union representative that he would ask the Union to identify its items of highest priority when the joint session continued. He suggested that this time be used to discuss the Union's priorities, if necessary.

When meeting with the Employer committee, the Mediator learned that while those present had some latitude as to settlement on cost items, past an undisclosed point further authority would have to be sought from the Opera's governing board. The committees were then brought together to continue the joint session.

Identify most important issues
<10>

MEDIATOR: Well, now I think I understand, at least factually, what's on the table. Since most of these proposals concern Union demands, I would like the Union to identify for all of us which of these it considers most important.

UNION REPRESENTATIVE: Everything that's on the table at this point is extremely important. I don't want to belittle any of our proposals.

MEDIATOR: Neither do I, but it makes sense to tackle the most important issues first. Where should we begin?

UNION REPRESENTATIVE: The number one issue so far as the Union is concerned is the topic of pensions.

MEDIATOR: I've looked at your expiring agreement, and I saw that you have a pension plan. What exactly is the problem that causes you to make pensions a top priority this year? Is there something about the existing plan that's not working well?

UNION REPRESENTATIVE: The current retirement benefits have only been in the agreement for a short while. As a result, there are quite a few musicians with lengthy service who will have a very small benefit when they retire. The entire orchestra, young and old alike, feel very strongly that these people should have some form of supplementary benefit. It just doesn't make sense that those who have done the most for the orchestra will get the least.

Don't allow positions to harden—focus attention on common concerns when possible
<11>

EMPLOYER REPRESENTATIVE: We are *not* going to pay these people for the rest of their lives. We just don't have the money to even think about that.

MEDIATOR: Hold it. Let's slow down a bit. What's your view about the basic problem they've mentioned. Should something be done for these people? I'm not asking whether you agree to pay them for the rest of their lives. Do you agree that their years of service ought to be rewarded in some way? They've said the existing pension plan only takes account of years worked *after* it went into effect.

A CASE STUDY 13

EMPLOYER REPRESENTATIVE: They're right about how the plan works, and we are not totally insensitive to that problem. The proposal we have on the table includes continuation of health insurance coverage for retirees. We think that will be very beneficial for long-service employees retiring now who will receive a comparatively small pension benefit. Given the financial condition of the Opera, however, there is no way we can agree to supplement monthly benefits forever.

Allow exploration of options <20>

UNION REPRESENTATIVE: We are not necessarily looking for a supplement to monthly benefits. We're just looking for some kind of payment that will recognize the service put in by those who will be retiring in the near future. It could take the form of a one-time lump sum payment, it could take the form of an annuity purchased by the Opera or any number of other things.

Highlight common ground for settlement <11>

MEDIATOR: It sounds to me as though the Employer has recognized the need to do something for the people in this group, that is, long-service employees who will be retiring in the near future. It also sounds to me as though the Union is very flexible about the form of a benefit that would satisfy its needs in this area. I am going to ask the Employer to take the time between now and our next meeting to put together a precise proposal in this area. Determine what you can spend and propose the form in which you would like to spend it. That will give us a starting point for further discussions.

Push for progress on specifics <14>

UNION REPRESENTATIVE: The second issue of critical importance to the musicians is wages. Now, you're going to need some detailed background here. Right now, the contract guarantees the musicians that they will be employed for specified periods of *time*. The musicians are guaranteed 20 weeks of employment during the regular season, 12 preliminary days, and 80 rehearsal hours. As a matter of fact, all the musicians make more than is guaranteed through this system as the result of overtime and extra events.

MEDIATOR: Let me make sure I understand. Does

the current contract guarantee earnings in any particular amount?

UNION REPRESENTATIVE: No, and that's the problem. All of the contract guarantees are stated in terms of time: 20 weeks, 12 days, and 80 hours. This creates a hardship for many of the musicians. They know that they are going to make more than the time guarantees in the contract suggest. But this is no help to them if they want to buy a home or make some other major purchase. They can't put the *time* guarantees down on a loan application, and they don't have any way to predict reliably what their precise income is going to be.

The contract needs something in addition to the time guarantees. We are asking to add a dollar guarantee for each year so that everyone can rely upon that as a minimum. And it should reflect more than just the guaranteed time, because all the musicians work more than that.

EMPLOYER REPRESENTATIVE: You know, the problem here is not clear to me. Everyone agrees the musicians are getting *more* than required by the time guarantees.

UNION REPRESENTATIVE: If this Opera wants to maintain a steady, professional orchestra, they are going to have to include a wage guarantee in the agreement that is clear and simple and reaches a livable level. These people are professionals and when they fill out a mortgage application, they ought to be able to represent with assurance that they will be making, for example, $30,000 per year. We've proposed that the new contract contain financial guarantees of $30,000 in the first year, $34,000 in the second year, and $38,000 in the third year.

EMPLOYER REPRESENTATIVE: I can't fault the musicians for wanting what has been proposed. But we had better not lose sight of certain basic facts. In the first place, the Opera has never suggested to any musician that it can offer full-time employment. Nearly all of the musicians do have other sources of income both during and outside the season, and they are not looking to the Opera to generate their entire annual incomes. Moreover, if the wealth were there to be shared, we would share it. But there simply is no wealth to be shared. It's no secret that the Opera has suffered extreme financial losses in recent years.

UNION REPRESENTATIVE: Look, I was asked to name the issues that *must* be dealt with to get a settlement, and this is the second one I've named. You might want to keep that in mind.

EMPLOYER REPRESENTATIVE: The Opera wants to maintain a steady, professional orchestra, and its actions make that evident. As you yourself have acknowledged, the Opera generates substantial income for nearly all of the musicians above and beyond the time guarantees in the contract. We could explore putting some language in the contract that would more clearly describe the amount that the musicians are earning. But don't be misled. There is no way that we can include some form of guarantee that might cause the Opera to pay money out without receiving services. There is nothing extra in the kitty for that.

> Encourage concrete proposals after exploratory discussion
>
> <14>

MEDIATOR: Why don't you develop some language for our next session that would describe the concept you are talking about. For now, simply leave the amounts blank. That will give us a chance to determine whether we can agree on an approach for dealing with wages under the new agreement.

EMPLOYER REPRESENTATIVE: All right, I'd be happy to do that.

UNION REPRESENTATIVE: There are a few things I want you to be thinking about when you prepare your new wage proposals. I've been hearing now for several months that these musicians cannot make a livable wage because the Opera is losing money. The musicians are not the ones responsible for raising money. That's your job. And they are certainly not the ones that have caused more to be spent in recent years than was received. If management did its job as well as the orchestra does its job, you wouldn't have a deficit.

EMPLOYER REPRESENTATIVE: Do you want to take over the Opera? Is that what you are suggesting? I don't see that here in any of the 19 proposals.

UNION REPRESENTATIVE: Well, we could probably do a better job of it. While we're on that topic I should highlight another proposal that is absolutely vital to our membership. We want the right to refuse to work with the harassing maestros you use to conduct some of the operas.

EMPLOYER REPRESENTATIVE: You want the right to veto the maestros we select to conduct the operas? Forget it! We will never agree to that!

UNION REPRESENTATIVE: We'll see about that! And some of the other contract language proposals we have made are critical too.

MEDIATOR: All right, let's cool it. Retiree benefits and wages are two very major items. Let's work on those in the manner I suggested before getting all riled up over anything else.

Further Developments: At this point, everyone agreed that in light of scheduling difficulties, no formal meeting could take place on Day 2. Day 2 was, therefore, set aside for the parties to further review their positions and for the Employer to develop the two specific proposals sought by the Mediator. It was agreed that the parties would meet with the Mediator and their full committees at 10:00 A.M. on Day 3.

Summary of Events
(Day Number 1; Joint and Private Sessions)

The Mediator began with a joint session. During the early parts of that session, the Mediator: (1) encouraged a ban on media releases; (2) explained alternate processes (such as orthodox arbitration and med-arb) that the parties might need to consider at later stages; and (3) emphasized that changes in position by both parties would be necessary to produce agreement.

Thereafter, the Mediator: (1) listened to full explanations from both sides regarding their positions on the outstanding issues; (2) took a break from the joint session to meet with each committee privately; (3) identified the most important issues; (4) asked questions to clarify the precise nature of problems; (5) allowed exploration of alternate solutions; (6) highlighted common ground offering a possible basis for settlement; and (7) encouraged preparation of concrete new proposals.

The Mediator met with each committee separately in order to get an impression of each committee member and the personal priorities that might play a part in any effort to reach a settlement, to determine if any absentee decision-makers would play a part in the negotiations, and to acquaint the participants with his experience.

The Mediator's objectives during the first session were: (1) getting to know the cast of characters; (2) setting a positive tone; and (3) educating himself about the issues. He was patient and heard full explanations of all positions from the parties. He did not become highly active in making suggestions, but rather sought to gain the confidence of both sides by listening to them and by acquainting the participants with his experience as a mediator.

When the discussion evidenced common ground that could lead to settlement, however, he did push for progress through development of new, concrete proposals. Before the next session, he will study all material he has received in order to learn all background facts that might be helpful in encouraging settlement.

The results of the session were discussed in the following conversation:

Private Conversation 5:00 P.M.

MEDIATOR: What did you think of the meeting?

OBSERVER: I was very interested by how you began. Do you always give the parties a "pep talk?"

MEDIATOR: Generally, yes. It's important to set the right tone. The parties need to believe that this is the time to trim the fat from their proposals. They won't do that unless they are convinced that movement can and *will* produce a settlement.

OBSERVER: Are your opening comments always the same?

MEDIATOR: I always ask for a ban on media campaigns if the dispute is in the news. Beyond that, what I say depends on the experience of the parties. These parties have used mediation before so I didn't need to explain the most basic things to them.

OBSERVER: What sorts of things might you cover with less-experienced parties?

MEDIATOR: If parties have never used mediation, I spend a little more time making sure all the participants know that I cannot impose a solution, that no settlement will be produced unless they agree to it.

OBSERVER: Anything else?

MEDIATOR: Yes. Sometimes it's a good idea to make clear that I will be meeting with each side privately, as well as calling joint meetings, that I will ask each side to speak to me confidentially, and that I will not disclose what I learn unless I have their permission.

OBSERVER: Is there ever any difficulty with those items?

MEDIATOR: I've never encountered any. Even though these things are not controversial, when parties have never used mediation before, it can be useful to have them sign an agreement stating all the ground rules. It can set a positive tone if parties that have been at loggerheads are at least able to sign the same piece of paper.

OBSERVER: Do you include anything special in the agreement?

MEDIATOR: It's important to check the law of the state where the mediation is taking place. Sometimes special language must be included to assure that the sessions will be confidential.

What did you think of the discussion on the issues?

OBSERVER: Two things surprised me. First, it surprised me that both sides displayed as much flexibility as they did on the pension issue. It sounds to me like they should have been able to accomplish more on that topic at the bargaining table.

Be sensitive to timing—note when *"pressure points"* are likely to motivate change

<21>

MEDIATOR: Sometimes, there is no substitute for the passage of time in negotiations. Both sides are looking at a deadline 13 days from now. If there is to be any movement, it's got to come now. And there is no question that parties behave differently in the presence of a third party than they do without that third party. They wouldn't have asked me to come in if they didn't want me to do some pushing and prodding before we are through. Parties want their position to seem fair to the person who is going to be pushing and prodding. What's the other thing that surprised you?

OBSERVER: Both sides seemed very conciliatory during nearly all of the meeting. Then, at the very end, tempers seemed to flare up and some less than fully constructive things were said. I was surprised that happened, and I was also surprised that you let them do it, rather than cutting off the banter immediately.

MEDIATOR: I am surprised to hear you use the words "let them." These negotiations belong to the parties, you know, not to me. It's very important for the parties to communicate their perceptions to one another, and I don't want to stand in the way of that. There will come a time when I will take charge to a greater extent. But initially, the parties have the right to educate me about the issues and, just as important, their feelings, in the way that they see fit. If I don't listen to them now, and assure them that I have heard out their concerns, I can't expect them to take kindly to my pushing and prodding later on.

Be *patient*—*listen* before trying persuasion
<21>

A mediator must have a great deal of patience. This attribute is particularly necessary at the beginning of the mediation. The mediator, of course, is in fact a third party to the negotiation, but the parties have to become used to that fact first, and the mediator must be careful not to take a position which would indicate that he or she is taking over the negotiation. One of the most difficult tasks for a mediator is determining the right time to begin actively pushing and prodding. It's impossible to give you any clear-cut rules about timing, but it's critical. If the mediator becomes too active before gaining the parties' confidence, the mediation is not likely to be successful.

OBSERVER: I've watched you act as an arbitrator, and sometimes you control the direction of the hearing very actively from the beginning.

MEDIATOR: That's right, but that's an entirely different role. As an arbitrator, I have an obligation to keep the parties focused on relevant, reliable evidence that is not repetitive. It's part of my job to make sure the proceeding is no more long and costly than it needs to be. But my role as a mediator is quite different. I *must* listen patiently in the beginning if I want the parties to listen to me later on. What's said may seem irrelevant or emotional, but sometimes participants in a negotiation need to vent a few things before confronting the essential issues. And it pays off to listen while they're doing this venting. I learn what's griping each side and it helps me to figure out what problems the settlement will have to address.

OBSERVER: Let me ask one more thing about this. I have read that some people advise a mediator *never* to persuade or argue with parties because that type of behavior makes the parties afraid of sharing information with a mediator who may have an axe to grind. What is your view on that?

Be neutral, but do *not* be "neutered"
<19>

MEDIATOR: That makes no sense whatsoever. Sometimes, parties in mediation settle because they develop a better appreciation for the other side of the story. Sometimes you can solve a dispute just by coming up with a new idea. But frequently, after these avenues have been exhausted, a few mountains still have to be moved. I have never found that anyone stops sharing information when I start to move those mountains. Of course, as I've already said, I don't start to take an active part in that way until I've patiently listened to the parties' positions and their gripes. When I start to push, they know they are listening to someone who is *fully* educated about their situation and able to bring considerable experience to bear on the problem. Timing is the most important element. I think you'll see what I mean as things develop.

OBSERVER: I see your point. What are you going to do between now and the meeting on Day 3?

Review any prior contracts and all proposals
<11>

MEDIATOR: The parties have, at my request, supplied me with quite a lot of paperwork. It includes a copy of the old agreement and full copies of the precise proposals on the table from each party at this time. I am going to go over all of these materials in detail.

OBSERVER: Why do you need to go over the old agreement? It seems like a waste of time to go over sections that neither side wants to change.

MEDIATOR: Continuing provisions from the old agreement could well affect the positions of the parties on the outstanding issues.

OBSERVER: Can't you rely on one side or the other to bring that up when it occurs?

Learn the background as well or better than the parties
<11>

MEDIATOR: I suppose if each side's representative was 100% effective 100% of the time, I could. But that's not going to happen. One of the reasons mediation can be effective is that the mediator can help a party understand their *own* proposals better. Maybe all of the ramifications haven't been thought through. Bringing new facts or new analysis to bear can cause one or the other side to change its position. In order to do the best possible job, therefore, a mediator should know the relevant facts as well or better than the parties.

Day Number 3

Meeting with Employer Representative
9:45 A.M.

MEDIATOR: Before beginning the joint meeting, I wanted to check with you. Were you able to put together a new pension proposal?

EMPLOYER REPRESENTATIVE: We have something, but I'm not sure it should be put out on the table.

MEDIATOR: Why not?

EMPLOYER REPRESENTATIVE: We're prepared to spend some money on the people who have been with us the longest, but I'd like to hold that back until the deadline is closer. They always try to get a little more from us at the end, and I don't want to be in the position of having spent everything in the bank too early.

MEDIATOR: We have 19 issues to deal with in about 10 days and, if we don't start making some progress somewhere, there won't be any settlement so you won't have to worry about spending anything!

EMPLOYER REPRESENTATIVE: Do we have to start with such a big ticket item?

MEDIATOR: Look, they've identified this as their highest priority, and you've stated that you recognize the need to do something for the long-service employees. That means that it ought to be possible to make some progress on this issue. If we make progress on their highest priority, it will be easier to deal with the other issues. That will generate some confidence in the mediation process.

EMPLOYER REPRESENTATIVE: I wish there were some way to avoid putting this proposal out there immediately.

MEDIATOR: It's your decision. You can avoid putting the proposal out there, but that also may "avoid" an opera season! In my judgment, you should back up your statement that something ought to be done for these people. Now is the time to move. The mediation has just begun, and they need to see that you are ready to work on a settlement. If they see that, they'll get down to business as well.

EMPLOYER REPRESENTATIVE: All right. Let's join the rest. I'll give you the proposal.

Joint Session 10:00 A.M.
(All Committee Members Present)

MEDIATOR: I asked the Employer to prepare a new proposal regarding supplementary retirement benefits for retiring employees with lengthy service. Have you been able to come up with anything?

EMPLOYER REPRESENTATIVE: We worked very diligently on this yesterday, and I think we are in a position to propose something that should fully address the union's needs. Before I describe that proposal, I want to emphasize something for everyone's understanding. We are not going to throw out a couple of peanuts, expecting to dicker back and forth until a little bit more is out on the table. As I said the other day, we recognize that the union's concerns in this area have some validity. The proposal that I am about to describe is a highly generous one, and we expect it to fully address those concerns. The proposal, which I will now distribute in writing, essentially contains the following provisions:

1. Any orchestra member who reaches the age of 70 and has 30 years of service may voluntarily retire;
2. Such a voluntary retiree will receive a supplementary retirement payment equal to 50% of their weekly salary during the last year of service multiplied by total years of service, not to exceed 40 years;
3. Only two such payments will be made during each contract year. Preference among those seeking voluntary retirement will be based upon seniority with the orchestra.

UNION REPRESENTATIVE: Let me ask one basic thing if I may. Does this benefit supplement anything that would be payable under the existing contract pension plan or take the place of it?

EMPLOYER REPRESENTATIVE: The existing contract pension plan stays in place. This is a supplemental benefit. It's designed to take care of the problem you have identified: people with lengthy service who don't qualify for much under the plan because it hasn't been in effect very long.

MEDIATOR: I am going to ask the Union committee to caucus and study this proposal carefully. When you have determined what your questions or responses will be, let me know. I'll be in my office. There is also a separate caucus room available for the Employer committee.

Private Conversation 11:00 A.M.

OBSERVER: Why didn't you say anything about the proposal before sending the parties in to caucus? It looks like the Employer is making some movement.

MEDIATOR: Nothing would be gained by commenting before the Union has had an opportunity to raise questions or comments. I need to hear further from the parties before I can judge whether this proposal has a chance of settling the issue.

OBSERVER: What do you plan to do when the Union reports back to you after their consideration of the Employer proposal?

Consider using "shuttle diplomacy"
<4>

MEDIATOR: My opinion could change, but right now I think that I will keep the parties in separate rooms and shuttle back and forth between them.

OBSERVER: The joint session this morning was fairly brief. Is there any particular reason that you expect not to continue meeting in joint session?

MEDIATOR: Joint meetings can accomplish several very important things. Initially, both sides need to explain their positions in the presence of the other. This is true for a couple of reasons. First, there are frequently people present who simply need to be assured that their grievances or concerns have been fully aired.

OBSERVER: Is that part of the reason you emphasize the need for patience?

MEDIATOR: Precisely. Secondly, there is always some prospect that during joint discussions one side will persuade the other that it has a valid point of view.

Sometimes, disputing parties have not really listened to each other before mediation. If they have spoken, their minds were busy planning their own next argument instead of listening. When I require each participant to avoid interruption while the other explains their views to me, things frequently start to sink in for the first time.

In this case, however, those benefits have already been secured through our joint session on Day 1. The Employer has agreed with the Union's point that something ought to be done for retirees with lengthy service.

OBSERVER: Can joint meetings accomplish anything at this stage?

Joint meetings may:	MEDIATOR: If we discover that there is some factual area relevant to a dispute that the parties have not explored, a joint meeting might be helpful in establishing the pertinent facts.
	OBSERVER: What sort of factual question might come up?
1. Assist in establishing relevant facts <4>	MEDIATOR: For example, where this issue is concerned, a question might come up as to how many people are likely to be interested in the voluntary retirement provision in the near future and what their individual benefit levels would be. A joint meeting might be useful in flushing out those facts so that everyone would be operating with common information as the mediation continued.
	OBSERVER: Is there anything else that joint meetings accomplish in the later stages of mediation?
2. Produce new ideas <20>	MEDIATOR: Yes. Sometimes, the parties are at a logjam on a particular issue, and I can't come up with any creative solution to get past that logjam. When that happens, I will sometimes call for a joint session just to get the parties talking and see if the brainstorming produces anything.
	OBSERVER: Does that really work?
	MEDIATOR: Yes. I recall one money claim I mediated outside the labor field. The claiming party was asking for over $600,000 and the responding party had only offered $10,000. I wasn't getting anywhere, so I called a joint session for the reasons I just described. The parties talked around the problem at some length. In the middle of that conversation, the responding party blurted out across the table, "Listen, could this thing be settled for $250,000?" The complaining party said no at the time, but the claim was ultimately settled for a figure very close to that amount. In other words, just keeping the parties talking produced some information that helped lead to a settlement. Before that was said, the complaining party was ready to give up on the process and simply litigate its claim to conclusion.
	OBSERVER: How does all of this bear on what you will do in this mediation right now?

26 THE ANATOMY OF MEDIATION

Shuttle diplomacy may produce more movement
<4>

MEDIATOR: None of the things that a joint session can accomplish are what is needed right now in this case. The Employer has put something out there which is substantially more than it had offered before mediation began. I hope and expect that the union is going to be willing to do some moving in response to that. I think both sides will be most likely to change their positions if they can talk to me in confidence about changes they are contemplating and the likelihood that those changes will successfully produce settlement of the issue. It is no secret that many times parties who are dealing directly with each other across the table hold back because they aren't sure whether they will get anything in response for a concession. If I engage in "shuttle diplomacy," I hope to get each side to disclose some possible room for movement that would not otherwise be disclosed.

OBSERVER: Were you thinking through all those considerations during the brief joint session?

MEDIATOR: Not exactly. But I've been doing something from the beginning that helps me decide how to proceed right now.

Determine timing by:

As I mentioned before, a mediator's most difficult task is judging timing—what's the right time to move from joint meetings to shuttle diplomacy? What's the right time to begin more actively pushing the parties toward a possible basis for settlement? When should the mediator initiate a concrete proposal that hasn't come from either side? When should the parties be kept at the table, and when might a break in the talks be helpful? Many people would say that timing decisions like these are simply handled by intuition, but I think there's more to it than that. My timing decisions are guided by the signals I receive from the conduct and statements of the parties.

Paying close attention to signals from the parties
<21>

OBSERVER: What do you mean by signals you get from the parties? Are you talking about something they consciously do to let you know what they want?

MEDIATOR: No, no, no. Let me explain with examples. When I met with the Union committee on

Day 1, the comments of the "old-timers" signaled to me that their key interest is retiree benefits. And the comments of the "young bucks" signaled to me that their key interest is wages. Now that could easily create some tension as we discuss the pension issue because the money pot may not be big enough to satisfy both groups fully. If I'm meeting privately with each committee, I'll be in a much better position to sense that tension and deal with it than I would be if we were meeting in joint sessions.

And I can give you another example. In our joint session, the Employer representative's comments clearly signaled that the Employer believes it has made substantial movement and is entitled to expect substantial movement in response. At this stage, I think that is an accurate belief. And I will be in the best position to get substantial movement from the Union committee if I meet with it separately.

Further Private Conversation 3:00 P.M.

OBSERVER: The Union has been caucusing over that proposal for an awfully long time. Don't you think you should find out what's happening?

MEDIATOR: Not necessarily. At a later stage of this mediation, I might be more apt to stick my head in the door and find out what's happening. At this stage, however, all of the Union committee members have just met me, and they haven't had an opportunity to get completely comfortable with my participation as yet. I don't want to disrupt the free flow of discussion in that room. I want to let them get as much as possible accomplished before I intervene.

Meeting With Union Committee 3:30 P.M.

UNION REPRESENTATIVE: All right, we have a comprehensive response to the Employer's proposal which has three parts. First, in terms of what the Employer put out on the table, we have no problem with Part 1 (eligibility) and Part 3 (yearly limit on participation), as long as one thing is clarified. We understand that the yearly limit will be cumulative over the life of the contract.

MEDIATOR: What do you mean by that?

UNION REPRESENTATIVE: What we mean is that if no one uses the voluntary retirement benefit in the first year of the contract, then four people could use it in the second year of the contract and so on. The only change we feel is absolutely necessary in the three part plan that the Employer put on the table has to do with the level of benefits. So far as we're concerned, these people deserve 100% of their weekly salary times years of service up to a maximum of 40 years.

> **Get simple explanations making clear the significance of proposals**
> <13>

MEDIATOR: All right. Let me ask this. What is the difference between the two proposals in dollars? Can you compare for me how each would work in the case of a particular musician?

UNION REPRESENTATIVE: Sure. Let's take some figures and work through an example. Let's suppose someone retires next year after 45 years with the Opera and he's making $1000 a week. We'll use that figure because it keeps the math simple. Under their formula, using the 50%, you start by chopping that $1000 in half. Then you multiply the $500 by 40. You can't use his extra five years of service because there's a cap at 40 years. So, this retiree would get a one-time payment of 40 times $500, or $20,000.

MEDIATOR: That's under the Employer proposal, correct?

UNION REPRESENTATIVE: Right. Now we're only proposing one difference. In the example I just talked about, we say don't begin by chopping the $1000 in half. Use 100% of his weekly earnings. We'll agree to exclude his last 5 years of service. But the 40 should be multiplied times the full $1000 for a payment of $40,000 in this case.

MEDIATOR: Which is exactly twice as much as the Employer proposed.

UNION REPRESENTATIVE: That's what it turns out to be, yes.

Firm up areas of agreement

<14>

MEDIATOR: I take it then that the format the Employer proposed is completely acceptable, although you want figures producing more money. Is that it?

UNION REPRESENTATIVE: Yes, but don't forget the clarification we want where the yearly limit on participation is concerned. There are some topics related to this Employer offer that we need to talk about. We can't really evaluate whether this one-time payment is going to be acceptable unless we've pinned down what the regular benefits for all retirees will be. There were some proposals outstanding on that before mediation began. At that stage, the Employer was proposing continued medical coverage for retirees, continuation of insurance for retirees' musical instruments, and two tickets for each retiree to the dress rehearsal for each performance. We want to make sure that all of that is still part of the package. We don't know what they intended, but so far as we're concerned, continued medical coverage for the retiree should include the retiree's spouse.

MEDIATOR: All right, I'll find out where the Employer stands on those items.

UNION REPRESENTATIVE: Finally, we feel that certain items must be added to this package in order to wrap up a total settlement regarding retirement benefits that will cover *everything*, not just the one-time supplemental payments. We propose continuation of dental coverage for retirees as well, and an increase in the Employer's regular pension contribution rate. Right now the Employer is contributing 7½% of guaranteed earnings. We propose that this be raised to 8½% of *total earnings*. As you know, most of the musicians work considerable overtime and extra engagements above and beyond their guaranteed hours. Right now, no pension contribution is made on those extra hours.

MEDIATOR: Is that your full proposal?

UNION REPRESENTATIVE: No. There is one further addition that is very important. Our lawyer tells me that there are some decisions by the National Labor

Relations Board saying that an employer has no legal obligation to bargain with a union about continuing medical benefits for retirees. We don't want these cases to cause any problem in the future. For that reason, it's critical that the agreement contain a provision stating that retirees remain a part of the bargaining unit for all rights involving pension, medical and/or dental coverage.

MEDIATOR: All right, I'm going to take a few moments to prepare some notes summarizing your positions, and then I'll return to make sure that I have everything right.

Further Developments: The Mediator privately prepared the following notes summarizing the Union's counterproposal on the question of pension benefits:

Mediator's Notes
Union Counterproposal
Day Number 3/3:30 P.M.

I. Supplemental Retirement Benefit:
   1. Eligibility—Employer proposal OK (Age 70 and 30 years service)
   2. Level of Benefit—*100%* of weekly salary during the last year of service times total years of service up to a maximum of 40 years.
   3. Limit on Participation—OK (two per year) if cumulative over the life of the contract.
II. Additional Benefits Previously Offered for All Retirees:
   1. Continued medical coverage for retiree and spouse (unclear if coverage for spouse was previously offered)
   2. Continued musical instrument insurance for retiree
   3. Two tickets to the dress rehearsal for each performance
III. Additional Benefits Proposed for All Retirees:
   1. Continued dental coverage for retiree
   2. Retirees remain a part of the bargaining unit for all rights involving pension, medical and/or dental coverage.
IV. Regular Contribution Rate for All Retirees Under Current Plan:
   1. 8½% (an increase from current 7½%) of *total* earnings (that includes overtime and extra engagements).

While the Mediator was preparing these notes, the following conversation took place:

> OBSERVER: Why are you taking so long to do this right now? There's no agreement on any package as yet.

Avoid "errors in transmission"
<7>

> MEDIATOR: It is very important that there be no mistake or error if the Mediator is going to transmit a counterproposal to the other party. It could create real problems if the Mediator discussed with the other party something which the Union had not intended. As I've explained, meeting privately with the parties has great advantages, but it can do even greater damage if a mediator isn't very careful to avoid "errors in transmission." Therefore, time must be taken to make specific notes of what is to be transmitted, in this case, to the Opera.
>
> In addition, I'm using this time to begin sizing up the differences in position between the parties. I'm beginning to make judgments as to what I believe might be acceptable to the other party. While I won't express any of those judgments just yet, they will begin to guide my comments to the parties as we progress.

Further Developments: The Mediator then returned to the Union committee and confirmed verbally that his notes accurately summarized the Union's counterproposal. This process will be used throughout the mediation to assure correct relay of proposals and counterproposals, although all of the Mediator's notes are not included in this Case Study.

The Mediator next met with the Employer committee to discuss the Union's counterproposal. The Mediator did *not* show his notes to the Employer committee, but rather presented the counterproposal verbally. The reasons for that practice will be illustrated later. The Mediator's conversation with the Employer committee was as follows:

Meeting With Employer Committee 4:30 P.M.

> MEDIATOR: Obviously, I've been working with the Union committee for some time now, but I think I have some results to show for it. I've convinced the

Union to accept your format for providing a supplemental retirement benefit. And they will also accept fully your definition of eligibility (voluntary retirement at age 70 with 30 years service), as well as your proposed limit on participation (two per contract year) so long as one clarification is made. They suggest that the limit on participation be cumulative over the life of the contract.

EMPLOYER REPRESENTATIVE: What does that mean?

MEDIATOR: That simply means that if no musician elected to retire during the first year of the agreement, then four could receive the supplemental retirement benefit in the second year of the agreement and so on. Let me put it differently. You've agreed to make this payment for a maximum of six people, two each year for three years. They aren't changing the maximum; it's still six, but it could be four in the second year and two in the last or all six at the end.

EMPLOYER REPRESENTATIVE: I see.

MEDIATOR: The Union does have a counterproposal regarding the level of benefit to be provided. The Union proposes that the benefit be 100% of weekly salary during the last year of service times total years of service up to a maximum of 40 years. Now as I understand it, that means the only difference between you is the percentage. You are at 50% and they are at 100%.

EMPLOYER REPRESENTATIVE: You could say that is the "only" difference, but it's a whopping big one. They're proposing exactly twice as much as we have on the table. That's absurd. We calculated our costs carefully before we made this proposal, and we put something substantial out there in good faith. They're in a totally different ball park.

Emphasize progress that has been made

<5>

MEDIATOR: Calm down. There's agreement on the format that you proposed, and that's pretty substantial. Let me simply finish presenting their counterproposal, and then you can consider how you want to respond on the money question.

EMPLOYER REPRESENTATIVE: You mean to say there is more to their counterproposal?

MEDIATOR: Well, the next topic in the counter-proposal also concerns a matter of clarification. According to the Union, you had certain proposed benefits for all retirees on the table before the mediation began. They want to make certain that those proposals are still part of the package. The items they mentioned were: (1) continued medical coverage for the retiree and his or her spouse; (2) continued musical instrument insurance for the retiree; and (3) two tickets to the dress rehearsal for each performance.

EMPLOYER REPRESENTATIVE: Now, look. We were willing to propose those items before, but that doesn't necessarily apply now. We've put our money into this supplemental retirement benefit, and that's no small piece of change. We can't necessarily afford to do that *and* everything else that was previously proposed.

<Investigate factual support for positions taken
<11>>

MEDIATOR: Just how much expense is involved where these items are concerned?

EMPLOYER REPRESENTATIVE: Well, in all honesty, all of them are not big ticket items. Continuing the musical instrument insurance for retirees amounts to very little since it's accomplished through a group plan. And, of course, the tickets for dress rehearsals are not a cost item.

MEDIATOR: In that case, I would encourage you to consider this very carefully before you yank those items back. We have made substantial progress. You may not like the Union 100% proposal, but they have fully accepted your format for a supplemental retirement benefit. If you want them to come down from that 100% figure, then you had better make sure that they don't feel we are going backwards rather than forwards. In my experience, I would have to say that if you remove items that were on the table before the mediation began, they *will* feel that we are moving backward. Again, let me simply suggest that you consider this carefully before you give me a firm position to take back to them.

<Discourage stands that will outrage the other side
<16, 19>>

EMPLOYER REPRESENTATIVE: We'll certainly do that. May we meet among ourselves for a time?

MEDIATOR: Just one moment. The Union is also proposing two additional items. First, they are proposing continued dental coverage for all retirees.

EMPLOYER REPRESENTATIVE: You must be kidding. That on top of everything else? That is a "big ticket" item and you can tell them to forget it!

MEDIATOR: The other proposal has to do with the contribution rate under the existing plan. As I understand it, the current rate is 7½% of guaranteed earnings. The Union is proposing that be increased to 8½% of *total* earnings, which would include overtime and extra engagements.

EMPLOYER REPRESENTATIVE: Well, to be perfectly frank, we had assumed that we would have to begin making contributions on total earnings during this contract period. The other Employers that contribute to this plan contribute on that basis. And we have assumed that in our cost forecasts. That will result in a considerable increase for them, and there's no reason to increase the percentage above 7½% at the same time.

MEDIATOR: There is one last item that I need to cover. In light of some legal case the Union wants to include language stating that you will continue to negotiate regarding retiree benefits in the future. They are not asking for a commitment that any particular benefits will be maintained after the term of this agreement. They are simply asking for a commitment that you will remain willing to discuss retiree benefits. Toward that end, they have proposed including a sentence in the agreement stating, "Retirees remain a part of the bargaining unit for all rights involving pension, medical and/or dental coverage."

EMPLOYER REPRESENTATIVE: What do they mean to accomplish by making them part of the bargaining unit? Are they trying to include retirees in ratification votes?

MEDIATOR: I don't know if that was considered. That's not the objective that was discussed with me. I'll find out. But before I do, let me give you time to talk among yourselves before telling me precisely what I should report back to the Union. I do want to note that in my judgment an agreement can be reached on the pension items. You have made movement. The Union has made movement. Both of you are on a path that can resolve this issue. Success in doing so will create an atmosphere of settlement on other issues. Let's not lose such an opportunity.

Further Developments: The Mediator left the Employer committee and, a short while later, the Employer Representative asked him to rejoin their committee. At that time, the following conversation took place:

EMPLOYER REPRESENTATIVE: We have tried to heed your advice to the full extent possible. First, let me talk about the one-time supplemental payments. We will agree to clarify that the limit on participation will be cumulative over the life of the agreement. And we are willing to make some change in the formula for computing the benefit, although that change cannot be in the percentage figure. Changing the percentage is simply too costly. Instead, we would be willing to increase the maximum years from 40 years to 45 years.

MEDIATOR: Can you summarize what a retiree would get under your proposal?

EMPLOYER REPRESENTATIVE: First, they would get any benefits for which they qualify under the current contract pension plan. During the term of the new contract, they would also get the supplemental benefit we have been talking about. Now under our proposal, you compute that by starting with 50% of the musician's weekly salary at retirement, *not* 100%, as the Union is proposing. Then that figure is multiplied by the number of years of service up to a maximum of 45 years. We've raised the maximum, but we can't raise the percentage.

MEDIATOR: What about the three items that were on the table for *all* retirees before the mediation began?

EMPLOYER REPRESENTATIVE: In reliance upon your advice, we are willing to keep those proposals on the table. But we can only do that if they drop their demand for dental coverage. There is no chance of that change being made, and the sooner they recognize that the better.

MEDIATOR: All right. Let me make certain my notes are correct. Your present offer includes: (1) continued medical coverage for retirees and their spouses, correct?

EMPLOYER REPRESENTATIVE: Yes, our prior offer didn't make clear that spouses were included, but we are willing to go that far.

MEDIATOR: Fine, and (2) continued instrument insurance for retirees, and (3) two tickets to the dress rehearsal for each performance.

EMPLOYER REPRESENTATIVE: That's all correct.

MEDIATOR: And your position on the regular contribution rate for the current contract pension plan?

EMPLOYER REPRESENTATIVE: As I indicated before, we are willing to change from guaranteed earnings to total earnings. That means we will make a contribution to the pension plan for overtime and extra hours. It should result in a very substantial increase in contributions. We see no reason to increase the percentage at the same time that this change is being made to their benefit.

Now let's discuss the question of the language they want stating that retirees remain part of the bargaining unit. We're going to have to consult with our attorney before anything is finalized, but our current thinking is as follows. We have no objection to stating in writing that we will continue to discuss retiree benefits. That is, we have no objection as long as it is clear we are not committed to maintain or increase any particular benefit. The obligation involved is simply an obligation to talk about it, nothing more. But we won't accept any language that seems to suggest retirees will be participating in ratification votes. These negotiations are tough enough without involving a lot of people whose jobs would not be on the line.

MEDIATOR: All right, we have quite a few balls in the air right now, and I want to make sure my notes on your counterproposal are accurate.

Further Developments: The Mediator then confirmed the accuracy of the following notes:

Mediator's Notes

Employer Counterproposal

Day Number 3/4:30 P.M.

I. Supplemental Retirement Benefit:
   1. Eligibility—Agreed (Age 70 and 30 years service)
   2. Level of Benefit—50% of weekly salary during the last year of service times total years of service up to a maximum of 45 years.
   3. Limit on Participation—Agreed (two per year, cumulative over the life of the contract)
II. Additional Benefits and Terms For All Retirees:
   1. Continued medical coverage for retiree and spouse; and
   2. Continued musical instrument insurance for retiree; and
   3. Two tickets to the dress rehearsal for each performance; *if*
   4. Demand for dental coverage *dropped.*
   5. Language saying Employer will continue to discuss retiree benefits—OK, *if* retirees do *not* participate in ratification votes.
III. Regular Contribution Rate For All Retirees Under Current Plan:
   1. 7½% of *total* earnings (that includes overtime and extra engagements).

After the accuracy of these notes was confirmed, the Mediator met with the Union committee.

Meeting with Union Committee 5:00 P.M.

MEDIATOR: Well, let me begin here. It was quite a struggle in there, but I finally convinced them to keep their previous offers for continued medical coverage, instrument insurance, and tickets on the table, *if* you remove your demand for dental coverage. I also talked them into extending the medical coverage to the retiree's spouse.

COMMITTEE MEMBER: But we were talking about a total package. We were willing to accept their form of supplemental retirement pay *if* we received the benefits, including dental, that we talked about. I don't want to give up something without knowing what my total package will look like. If we give up the dental benefits will the payment be figured on a 100% basis rather than a 50% basis?

Isolate fair exchanges that can be made

<16>

MEDIATOR: Let's put aside the formula right now. I know that you're interested in what the package will look like, but it makes sense to isolate certain issues and see if we can get agreement upon them. After all, you can't win a war without fighting battles. You can count on continued medical coverage for the retiree *and spouse*, instrument insurance, and dress rehearsal tickets if you withdraw the dental coverage demand. I suggest you think about it. Continued medical coverage for the retiree and spouse is an attractive benefit. If I were in your shoes, I'd give top priority to wrapping up the deal on that. It's worth dropping the dental now, because you really can't expect them to buy that much added cost at one time. It seems like a good exchange to me.

UNION REPRESENTATIVE: We'll discuss that. We may be able to withdraw that request for now, if we have the language stating that they will discuss retiree benefits in the future.

MEDIATOR: Well, they had some question about that language, but I think we can resolve the issue. I explained what you had said, but they expressed confusion as to precisely what you're trying to accomplish. In particular, they expressed some fear as to whether you intend to have retirees participate in contract ratification votes in the future. In that case, they would oppose putting the language in the agreement.

UNION REPRESENTATIVE: They don't have any right to tell us how to run ratification votes.

MEDIATOR: No one is suggesting that they do. They just want to know what your intentions are. We may or may not have any problem here. Had you contemplated using this to permit retirees to participate in contract ratification votes?

UNION REPRESENTATIVE: That had absolutely nothing to do with the proposal. As a matter of fact, under the Union bylaws, retirees would not be eligible to participate in any contract ratification vote.

MEDIATOR: If that's the case, then I'm pretty sure we can get some agreement on this front. Assuming we get this language worked out, will you drop the dental coverage demand for an assurance on continued medical coverage, instrument insurance, and rehearsal tickets? I'll step outside a moment so you can talk about it. It makes sense to me.

> Ask about intentions in order to avoid conflict
>
> <12>

Further Developments: Only a brief discussion outside the presence of the Mediator was necessary. During that time, the following discussion took place between the Observer and the Mediator:

OBSERVER: You did something and I'm wondering if you did it on purpose or if it just happened that way.

MEDIATOR: What's that?

OBSERVER: All of the prior discussions started with the formula for the supplemental money benefit. During this last meeting with the Union committee you began with different items. You started with the fringe benefits for *all* retirees. Was that intentional?

MEDIATOR: Absolutely. I saw the trade-off that I suggested as a fair one that they could accept. The Union has a chance to get a commitment on continued medical coverage for the retiree *and* spouse. That's attractive, and as I told them, it's just not realistic to expect dental insurance will be thrown in during the same negotiations. That's too large an increase in costs. The medical, along with the other benefits, the instrument insurance and tickets, is a good package that they should approve. I started with that because I wanted to get things moving in a positive direction, and wrap up as much as possible.

OBSERVER: You didn't say anything about the 50% versus 100%. Was that deliberate?

MEDIATOR: Yes. It looked to me like we could get an immediate agreement on the other items. I wanted to do so and then address the tougher problem of cutting the percentage figure. In short, I wanted the Union to begin to believe in the mediation effort by achieving agreement on some of the items that they raised.

The Mediator was then asked to rejoin the Union committee where the following took place:

UNION REPRESENTATIVE: O.K. You've got that part of the package. We'll drop the dental demand in exchange for medical, instrument insurance, and rehearsal tickets. Keep in mind, though, that's based on getting the language question worked out; we have to have a commitment that they *will* discuss retiree benefits in the future.

MEDIATOR: Understood.

UNION REPRESENTATIVE: Now where do we stand on the money items that are outstanding?

MEDIATOR: As to the formula for the supplemental benefit, the Employer feels it has to stick with 50%. Apparently, that's all the budget will bear, but I did get them to push the maximum up to 45 years of service.

UNION REPRESENTATIVE: So that would be 50% of the employee's weekly salary times years of service up to a maximum of 45 years?

MEDIATOR: Correct. As to the proposed change in the general level of pension contributions, they simply are not going to make two changes, both of which are likely to have clear impact, in the same year. In fact, they're very hesitant about *any* change in light of the new supplemental benefit that's now proposed. I think you need to talk among yourselves and decide which change is your highest priority. Is it more important to increase the 7½% or to get contributions on *total* earnings, including the overtime and extra work? I don't know that I can get either, but I know *both* are not likely to be in the picture. Think about it. The higher percentage may sound good, but going to total earnings may do more for you in the long run.

UNION REPRESENTATIVE: So what all do we need to talk about?

MEDIATOR: As far as I see it, the open issues that you need to think about are computation of the one time, supplemental payment for voluntary retirees and the contribution rate for general pension contributions. Why don't you take some time to talk about those two issues and report back to me.

Further Development: While the Mediator was waiting to hear further from the Union committee, the following discussion took place:

OBSERVER: I didn't want to interrupt, but I think you made a mistake.

MEDIATOR: What do you mean?

OBSERVER: When we were with the Employer committee, they said they *would* contribute to the general pension plan on *total* earnings. You didn't report that change to the Union.

MEDIATOR: That was *not* a mistake. The parties are quite a distance apart on the percentage that goes into the benefit formula. I think before we are done I'm going to need something to entice the Union to come down to a figure far closer to the Employer percentage. The Employer committee has shown no flexibility on that issue. If I threw out the change to total earnings right now, nothing would be accomplished, but later that concession may accomplish a great deal.

OBSERVER: Aren't you being a little bit dishonest?

MEDIATOR: Not at all. The Employer made that concession as part of a package that included agreement on *its* 50% formula for the supplemental benefit. That hasn't happened, so technically no concession has been made. And besides, I was retained to help these parties reach a settlement and that's precisely what I'm doing.

OBSERVER: Do you do that often?

MEDIATOR: Do what?

OBSERVER: Hold back movement that one or the other side is willing to make.

MEDIATOR: No, I don't. As I've already emphasized, timing is all important. There are all kinds of devices, but none are useful if they aren't used at the right time. This device, which some refer to as keeping a "pocket concession," is generally only useful if two things have happened. I have to have heard enough discussion to size up the range within which a settlement might be possible. And, just as important, I must have developed some notion as to who will have to move the furthest to get into that range. A so-called "pocket concession" can help get that movement.

OBSERVER: I see now why you haven't been relaying proposals by showing the parties your notes.

MEDIATOR: That's part of it. We just talked about the other reason for that. I need to control the order in which items are discussed. Sometimes there is good movement on one item and none on another. The order in which things are presented can help prevent either side from becoming too discouraged.

Further Developments: The Union representative reported to the Mediator changes of position on the two open issues. The Union proposed that the one-time supplemental payment for voluntary retirees be 75% of weekly salary times years of service up to a maximum of 40 years. This counterproposal demonstrated that the Union had no interest in raising the cap to 45 years, as suggested in the Employer's last offer, even though that change would be to the Union's benefit. The Union Representative reported that if only one change in contribution rate was possible, the change to *total earnings* was preferred. The Union also proposed that the general pension contribution rate be raised over the life of the contract by increasing it to 8% in the second year of the contract and 8½% in the third year of the contract.

Meeting With Employer Committee 5:30 P.M.

MEDIATOR: All right. We've made progress, but there's still work to be done. First, as to the one-time payment for voluntary retirees, the Union was not interested in raising the maximum years included in the computation to 45. They have, however, brought down their percentage proposal from 100% to 75%.

EMPLOYER REPRESENTATIVE: I don't see how we can monkey with the percentage and still stay within our budgetary constraints. Changing that puts us in a different ball park.

Suggest new approaches
<15>

MEDIATOR: Let me ask you this. The Union seems bent on getting some improvement in the percentage. The proposal I just came back with did not include the increase in maximum years from 40 to 45 that you had made available as part of the computation. That makes it pretty clear that they're looking for an increase in the percentage as opposed to any other part of the computation. Is there any way that you can increase the percentage by some amount and stay within your budget, perhaps by bringing the maximum years of service down a bit?

EMPLOYER REPRESENTATIVE: (After doing some figuring) It looks like we would be paying out roughly the same amount if we went with 60% of weekly earnings times years of service up to a maximum of 38 years.

MEDIATOR: That doesn't give me too much to work with. They've already come down 25% from 100 to 75. You're only coming up 10% from 50 to 60. Are you sure you can't do any better? I can try to work with the 60%, but I can't be very promising.

EMPLOYER REPRESENTATIVE: Look, we can't help it if they started with their heads in the clouds. And we're not willing to put the 60% on the table at this point. We're going to hold with 50% and 45 years of service. We feel a little bit more confident of our calculations with that proposal.

Highlight where movement is needed
<19>

MEDIATOR: I'll see what I can do, but I think some change in the percentage is going to be necessary to settle this. As to the language about retirees remaining part of the bargaining unit, I don't think we have any problem. They don't plan to have retirees participate in contract ratification votes. Their only purpose in proposing this is to make sure that you will not refuse to discuss continuation of various benefits for retirees in future negotiations.

EMPLOYER REPRESENTATIVE: Let me make sure I have this clear. We are only talking about the obligation to discuss benefits in the future. Right? We're not talking about any obligation to agree on particular benefits, are we?

MEDIATOR: They said they only want to make sure the Employer does not refuse to discuss these topics in the future.

EMPLOYER REPRESENTATIVE: Well, I can't see any problem in agreeing to that, as long as what we are agreeing to is made clear. This language is not clear.

MEDIATOR: What language would you suggest?

EMPLOYER REPRESENTATIVE: I'm not sure. I'd prefer that the Union propose new language.

MEDIATOR: On the last issue, namely, the general level of pension contributions, they have made some substantial movement. Rather than going to 8½% immediately, the Union proposes increasing to 8% in the second year of the agreement and 8½% in the third year of the agreement.

EMPLOYER REPRESENTATIVE: We had contemplated making some improvement in the contribution level later in the contract term, but I think they are moving it up too quickly.

Suggest new approaches
<15>

MEDIATOR: What about proposing a four-year agreement? You could keep 8% for the second and third year of the agreement and go to 8½% in the fourth year.

EMPLOYER REPRESENTATIVE: I like the notion of a four-year agreement. We're not interested in going through this any more frequently than necessary! We can go with 7½% in the second year, 8% in the third year and 8½% in the last year. That gets them where they want to be eventually.

MEDIATOR: All right, I'll see what I can do with this.

Meeting With Union Committee 6:00 P.M.

MEDIATOR: As you can see, I was with the Employer group for quite a while, and I think we're pretty close to the bottom of the barrel. As to the general level of pension contributions, I've gotten them to go for your figure, but they want a little bit longer to get there. They are proposing a four-year agreement with 7½% in the second year, 8% in the third year, and 8½% in the fourth year. They are also willing to agree to language clarifying that retiree benefits must be discussed in the future. The only place I have not gotten a change is on the benefit computation for the supplemental payment to voluntary retirees. As to that, they are holding with 50% and a maximum of 45 years.

UNION REPRESENTATIVE: I think we can sell this package to our membership if we can just get some change in the percentage part of the computation. People will think that 50% is simply too low.

Firm up areas of agreement

<14>

MEDIATOR: Then I take it you can go for the four-year agreement, reaching 8½% in the fourth year?

UNION REPRESENTATIVE: Assuming we take care of the other issues on the table satisfactorily.

MEDIATOR: Of course.

UNION REPRESENTATIVE: But what about the percentage; we've got to do something with that.

MEDIATOR: Let me ask you this. I think I can push them to 60% if the maximum years are brought down a bit, perhaps to, say, 38 or so. Is there any point in my pushing for that? Would that make it substantially more salable for you?

UNION REPRESENTATIVE: I'm not sure. Give us a chance to talk about it among ourselves.

UNION REPRESENTATIVE: (After a brief discussion outside the Mediator's presence) We don't feel good about the 60%. It's going to look low to our members. And for crying out loud, why should we move 40% down from our opening proposal when they're only coming up 10%?

MEDIATOR: Let me throw out an idea here. This may be totally beyond what I'm capable of getting, but I'll suggest it anyway. If I could get them to go for contributions on *total* earnings to the general pension plan, could you swallow the 60%. Changing to total earnings would benefit all musicians for a long time to come, you know.

UNION REPRESENTATIVE: Are we still talking about working up to 8½% by the fourth year of the agreement. Would that still be part of the package?

MEDIATOR: That's on the table now, yes.

UNION REPRESENTATIVE: That certainly gives us more to talk about. Give us a couple of minutes, here.

Authors' Comment: It should be observed that in this meeting, the Mediator is trying to push the Union committee to the 60% figure that was discussed during his last conversation with the Employer committee. The Mediator's strategy will be discussed in the private conversation between the Mediator and Observer that takes place at 7:30 P.M.

Further Developments: The Union representative reported that 60% up to 38 years and contributions of 7½%/7½%/8%/8½% on *total* earnings would settle all economic disputes regarding pension benefits. The meeting with the Union committee finished with the following brief discussion:

MEDIATOR: I'll do my best to put together this pension package, but I can't make any guarantees. As to the language clarifying that the parties will discuss retiree benefits in the future, they are concerned about the precise phrasing of the proposal you made. Can you suggest an alternative?

UNION REPRESENTATIVE: So far as we're concerned, what we proposed makes it clear enough. If they have a problem, they should make a suggestion.

Make specific proposals, if necessary

<23>

MEDIATOR: Let me ask you this. Does the following sentence address your concerns, "The issues affecting retirees are negotiable subjects in subsequent agreements"?

UNION REPRESENTATIVE: Yes, I think it does. If you can get that language and 60% in the payment computation, we've got a package we can agree upon.

Meeting With Employer Committee 6:15 P.M.

MEDIATOR: All right, I think we are at a point where a deal ought to be cut. First, let's cover the rate for contributions under the current pension plan. You have agreed to contributions on total earnings. They'll go for a four-year agreement with 7½% in the second year, 8% in the third year and 8½% in the last year, assuming, of course, that we resolve the other issues on the table. As to the language issue, they will go for the following sentence, which I think accurately expresses what both sides have been talking about, "The issues affecting retirees are negotiable subjects in subsequent agreements." Any problem with that?

EMPLOYER REPRESENTATIVE: That sounds acceptable. We can agree to that, subject to a check with our attorney.

MEDIATOR: Sure. Now, as to the last item, they have to have some increase in the percentage. If you can go with 60% and the 38-year limit that we talked about, we have a deal.

EMPLOYER REPRESENTATIVE: I told you before that we feel more comfortable with 50% and 45 years. I'm inclined to hold out for that.

MEDIATOR: Frankly, you had better be prepared to hold out for the duration of the opera season. The Union committee is convinced that 50% won't sell with the membership. It looks low, and that's not just their problem; it's your problem also. The added 10% will get you a settlement of all pension issues even if the cap on years is brought down to 38.

EMPLOYER REPRESENTATIVE: With 60% and a 38 year limit, the entire area of pensions is resolved?

MEDIATOR: That's absolutely right.

EMPLOYER REPRESENTATIVE: Well, under the circumstances, we can do it.

48   THE ANATOMY OF MEDIATION

Finalize agreements in writing immediately
<14, 24>

MEDIATOR: I think you've made the right decision. All right, I want to gather everyone together so that we can jointly annotate your original proposal with these changes. I want everyone to sign one document reflecting those changes and then we will distribute copies.

EMPLOYER REPRESENTATIVE: That's all right. But don't forget that we need to check with our attorney on that one item.

MEDIATOR: I haven't forgotten, but we want to make an immediate record of what we have discussed up to this point.

Further Developments: The parties met for the purpose of approving a memorandum of settlement as described by the Mediator. The Mediator, as indicated above, suggested working from the Employer's initial written proposal as a starting point since most of its items were part of the settlement. Changes and additions could efficiently be made to reflect the final agreement on pensions. The Mediator read each line, stated what changes seemed necessary, and sought each side's agreement that the words as changed accurately stated the deal. He then went through his notes and suggested each additional topic as to which language was needed. At this stage, the Mediator began by asking for suggested language from the parties. When the parties had difficulty, he put forth a simple statement of the agreement on that topic as he understood it. This process produced the document set forth below. The first three paragraphs are modified from the Employer's initial proposal. Italics indicate the modifications. The remainder was newly drafted.

Memorandum of Pension Settlement

1. Any orchestra member who reaches the age of 70 and has 30 years of service may voluntarily retire;
2. Such a voluntary retiree will receive a supplementary retirement payment equal to *60%* of their weekly salary during the last year of service multiplied by total years of service, not to exceed *38* years;
3. Only two such payments will be made during each contract year. Preference among those seeking voluntary retirement will be based upon seniority with the orchestra. *The number of per-*

mitted retirement payments shall be cumulative over the life of the contract if unused in any year.
4. Medical coverage for retirees and their spouses shall continue for the life of the contract.
5. Musical instrument insurance for retirees shall continue for the life of the contract.
6. Retirees are entitled to two tickets to all open dress rehearsals.
7. Issues affecting retirees are negotiable subjects in subsequent agreements.
8. The contribution rate for the regular pension plan will be applied to total earnings and will be as follows:
    Year 1—7½%
    Year 2—7½%
    Year 3—8%
    Year 4—8½%

After this document was created, the Employer's representative was excused to receive a return call from the Employer's attorney. A short while later, the Mediator was called into the room where this telephone call was taking place:

Meeting With Employer Committee 7:00 P.M.

EMPLOYER REPRESENTATIVE: Listen, we're having a bit of a problem. Would you please talk to our attorney?

MEDIATOR: Sure. (To the Employer attorney over the telephone) What seems to be the problem?

EMPLOYER ATTORNEY: I've told my client that I simply cannot advise them to agree on this language change. What they have read to me is, "The issues affecting retirees are negotiable subjects in subsequent agreements." The case law is very clear that they have no legal obligation to negotiate regarding retiree benefits.

Do not give legal advice to parties—they should have their own counsel

MEDIATOR: I haven't tried to give them any advice about their legal obligations. That's your job. But it's also true that your client has no legal obligation to have an opera season this year either! And, if they can't reach some kind of accommodation on this issue with the Union, there may be no opera season.

EMPLOYER ATTORNEY: I can't see how this language

could be that big of a deal. As I understand it from my clients, they have made some significant economic changes.

MEDIATOR: Well, you haven't been here, and you'll simply have to take my word for the fact that this language is a big deal as far as the Union is concerned. Some economic improvements have been made. All the Union wants is the assurance that the Employer will at least discuss continuation of these benefits in the future. It's been made very clear that this language does not obligate the Employer to enter into any particular agreement in future negotiations. It simply states that they will discuss continued benefits for retirees. Are you really willing to tell your client that they should blow up a settlement on this issue by refusing to simply discuss certain issues in the future?

EMPLOYER ATTORNEY: Well, I'm going to tell my clients that they should not agree to the language you recommend.

MEDIATOR: Let me get something clear. Are you going to advise them on the legal matters or are you, in effect, going to tell them what they should do with reference to the matters we are trying to settle?

EMPLOYER ATTORNEY: Well, I don't see the difference.

MEDIATOR: The difference is that whoever is making final decisions on the issues should be here participating. You don't think this language is a big deal, but if you had been here participating you would know that it *is* a big deal.

EMPLOYER ATTORNEY: Well, I told you what I'm going to do. What are you going to do?

MEDIATOR: I will talk to your clients and ask them if they want you to sit in on the negotiations. If so, I certainly have no objection. But I cannot conduct a mediation if people who are not directly involved in our meetings are going to tell one party or the other that they should or should not agree to certain matters. I don't object to your advising them about their legal rights, but I do object to your telling your clients that they should *not* agree to something, particularly when that something is necessary to settle an important issue in the negotiations. Unless this problem is worked out, there will be no settlement on the matter of pensions, retirees, or any other subject. I won't tell your clients the legalities of what is being suggested, but the fact is that what is being proposed is not illegal according to the information and advice that I have received, and the proposed language that I have on the table for the consideration of both parties would resolve the entire subject of pensions, which is one of the crucial matters in this present negotiation. If you personally want to take the responsibility for blowing up these negotiations, that's up to you. I'm going to talk to your clients now, I want you to know, and I'm going to tell them just what I have told you.

EMPLOYER ATTORNEY: That's certainly your prerogative, but let me finish my conversation with them first.

MEDIATOR: (After completion of the telephone call, to the Employer Committee) You heard what I said to your attorney, but let me emphasize a couple of things. First, it's very important that I know who is calling the shots. If they're being called by someone who's not here, then what we're doing is pretty pointless.

You, of course, may talk to your attorney, but I think I should know whether an attorney who sits in an office some distance from here is, in effect, going to be part of your negotiating team. I am entitled to know that and so is the Union. If you choose to have him in negotiations as part of your team, of course, you have a right to do so. But, as Mediator, I do not intend to carry out any further mediation with persons who are not here at the time that we are conducting a negotiation and seeking to arrive at an agreement. This is fundamental. A mediator cannot conduct mediation with unseen or invisible persons.

EMPLOYER REPRESENTATIVE: We have discussed this matter with our attorney, and we assure you that we are the ones who are going to decide what can be agreed to and will be agreed to.

MEDIATOR: All right, then let's get back to the issue at hand. I think it's up to all of you to decide whether you want a settlement of the pension issues or not. The fact is that the Union wants the assurance which my proposed sentence provides. It is my opinion, based upon legal advice given to me, that there is nothing illegal about it. In addition, it is customary in many agreements to have such a provision. Your concern was whether or not the retirees would in any way affect negotiations by having a right to vote, and the assurance has been given to you that they may not vote and will not vote in any future negotiations. The proposal simply provides that the Union will have the right in future negotiations to raise issues affecting retirees.

Your attorney has just explained to you that you don't have to agree to this language. As I pointed out to him, you also don't have to have an opera season. I think this language is a pretty small price to pay for a settlement of the whole pension issue. All the Union is asking you to do is agree that you will discuss certain topics with them in the future. You haven't committed yourself to anything other than good faith negotiations. How can you argue with that?

EMPLOYER REPRESENTATIVE: I guess we can't. The language stays in.

MEDIATOR: All right. Let's go back to the main meeting room. I want everyone to date and sign the memorandum we created.

EMPLOYER REPRESENTATIVE (while entering the main meeting room): Are you sure we should sign this? We don't have a contract yet and they'll need a ratification vote.

MEDIATOR: All we are doing is making a record of what has been discussed so far. No one will be bound if a full contract is not reached and approved. Those have been the ground rules from the beginning. But we don't want confusion about what's been done so far.

EVERYONE: All right.

MEDIATOR (after signing of the memorandum): Now, the other day when we were together, I asked you to take a shot at producing a new system for defining guaranteed wages. Were you able to come up with anything?

EMPLOYER REPRESENTATIVE: Yes, we have a proposal.

MEDIATOR: Let's take a break for dinner, and come back at 8:30 to work on that. I'll tell the Union committee what our schedule is.

Keep the pace moving when success is produced
<9>

Summary of Events
(Day Number 3; First Session)

The Mediator decided to pursue settlement of pension issues through shuttle diplomacy for two central reasons: (1) Competing interests of Union committee members concerning this issue, which could easily give rise to tensions, could best be handled in separate meetings, and (2) separate meetings seemed more likely to disclose what was in each party's "secret heart."

When presenting counterproposals to each committee separately, the Mediator promptly firmed up areas of agreement. He prepared careful notes after each separate meeting in order to be certain that no mistakes were made in transmission. The Mediator did not, however, show his notes to either party while working toward settlement. This was avoided, in part, so the Mediator could control the order in which topics were addressed.

Very early in the Day 3 meeting, the Mediator began to develop an impression in his mind regarding a basis for settlement of the pension issues which could be sold to both parties. He concluded (from the parties' positions and comments) that the percentage portion of the supplemental benefit formula would be the most crucial issue, and the most difficult to resolve. He also concluded that something greater than the Employer's initial proposal of 50% would be necessary to reach a settlement.

After the Mediator formed an impression regarding a basis for settlement, he became a third party to the negotiations, essentially acting on behalf of the settlement he had in mind and actively persuading both parties to move toward the settlement. He was far more assertive than he had been when educating himself about the issues.

He strongly advised the Employer *not* to remove retiree benefits that were previously offered from the table, and he pushed the Union to drop its request for dental coverage in exchange. He "smoked out" the information that the Employer could go to 60% if absolutely necessary. And he used that information, as well as a concession he had been saving (contributions on *total* earnings) to bring the Union to the point of settlement. On another occasion, the Mediator proposed specific language (future negotiation of retiree benefits) when the parties seemed to be in agreement, but could not state their agreement.

As soon as settlement of pension issues was accomplished, the Mediator insisted that it be reduced to writing and signed. When the settlement was threatened by the outside advice of the Employer's attorney, the Mediator *strongly* advised that all final decision-makers participate in the negotiations so that they might have the benefit of discussions there.

Finally, the Mediator sought to fully capitalize on the constructive mood created through settlement of all pension issues by working into the evening on wages.

The results of the session were discussed in the following conversation:

Private Conversation 7:30 P.M.

OBSERVER: Well, I've got a barrage of questions for you now. Things were really moving quickly this afternoon. I suppose my first question concerns precisely that fact. How were you able to get so much accomplished? The Union identified the topic of pensions as their number one priority, and after many negotiations the parties were not able to make any progress. Nonetheless, in one afternoon you cracked that nut. Are you sure there is nothing magical about mediation?

MEDIATOR: Yes, I am. Perhaps if you asked some of your other questions, we can flush out the answer to that question.

OBSERVER: That's a good idea. First, I'm curious about how you treated the Employer representative's statement that the Employer might agree to 60% and 38 years, *if* absolutely necessary to get a deal. As I understood it, the Employer was not putting that position out on the table during that conversation. The two of you were just discussing possibilities. And yet, in your next meeting with the Union committee, you suggested that you might, with further effort, be able to move the Employer to that point. You were clearly making use of the information the Employer had given to you. Don't mediators have some sort of obligation to keep information they are given by one party or the other confidential? Was what you were doing consistent with that obligation to keep information confidential?

Do not misunderstand the obligation of *confidentiality*
<7>

MEDIATOR: I'm very glad you've asked these questions. A great deal has been written and said about the obligation of mediators to keep information given to them confidential, and, quite frankly, I think a vast number of people are rather confused in this area.

There's no question that when a party gives a confidential explanation for their position, that explanation should not be disclosed. But that's not what happened today.

Frequently, as happened today, a party will make known that a change in position is possible, if absolutely necessary to reach agreement, even though that change is not currently being offered. That is, the party is not currently authorizing the mediator to communicate any change in position.

OBSERVER: Is that what happened here?

MEDIATOR: Yes. That happened when I first discussed the possibility of a 60%/38-year formula with the Employer committee. The Employer was willing to move to that formula if absolutely necessary to reach an agreement, but it did not authorize me to change the position it had outstanding on the table.

The mediator *should* make some use of this information. There is absolutely no point whatsoever in separating the parties and conducting "shuttle diplomacy," if no use whatsoever is made of the resulting information.

OBSERVER: So what use should be made of the information?

MEDIATOR: Assuming the disputed issue can't be settled without a further change of position, the mediator should find out whether the change that's being contemplated would be sufficient to settle the issue. Frequently, a party will be hesitant to make a final change in position unless that party *knows* that the change will be sufficient to get a settlement. The party may fear that, little by little, more and more will be exacted until the proposal has gone beyond the point of reason. In this circumstance, I explored with the Union committee whether it could finalize a settlement with a 60%/38-year formula. When I found that it could, that gave me the information I needed to secure that final change in position from the Employer.

Possible *changes* in position, related confidentially, *should* be used, but with care
<7>

Now, let me summarize what the bottom line is so far as this kind of information is concerned. When one side communicates a possible change in position on a confidential basis, it is neither proper nor useful to run over and immediately blurt out that change as absolute movement to the other side. But this does not mean the mediator should act as though he has never heard the information. To the contrary, the mediator should make use of the information when exploring possible bases for settlement with the other side. Using the information in that manner does not in any way breach any obligation of confidentiality. The mediator is simply using the information to find paths through which an agreement may be reached.

OBSERVER: So, you don't disclose the confidential position, but rather use it as a guide light showing a direction for possible settlement, is that it?

MEDIATOR: You're right on the button!

OBSERVER: I had a question about something else you did during today's session. When the parties could not come up with language representing their agreement on the question of issues affecting retirees being negotiable, you did not hesitate to propose specific language yourself. Isn't that a little bit risky? What if the parties get into a dispute later as to precisely what that language was intended to mean?

The mediator may draft proposals
<23>

MEDIATOR: Well, the mediator could certainly avoid all risk whatsoever by doing nothing, but I don't think that's advisable. When the parties agree upon a certain provision or condition, it is, of course, necessary to draft language reflecting as specifically as possible the agreement of the parties. In many instances, the mediator, as the result of experience, can aid the parties in drafting such language, and the mediator should do so. Where the parties seem to be in agreement on a particular matter but are unable to express the agreement in a manner that suits both of them, it is the mediator's function to draft language satisfactory to both parties that reflects the precise agreement.

Of course, the mediator should take steps to assure that proposed language doesn't create more problems later on. This can be accomplished by making certain that *the parties* explain their construction of the language to each other across the table before the deal is finalized. This assures that the settlement is framed by *the parties'* intentions and not the mediator's drafting thoughts.

OBSERVER: Why is it so difficult for people to put their agreement in written words?

MEDIATOR: Many times during mediation the parties remain suspicious of one another and they are unwilling to accept language proposed by the other party because they fear it has terms with unforeseen meaning. They may need help constructing neutral language that does not favor one party or the other. That's what happened today.

Sometimes, it can be trickier. On occasion, negotiating parties will resolve the crux of an important issue but will not be able to agree on some details. If they are willing to leave those details without resolution, in the hope that situations concerning them will never arise, then they will need to artfully craft language with "purposeful ambiguity" that expresses the agreement in concept without treading on the troublesome ground. An experienced mediator can help to craft such language.

In short, it is part of the mediator's function to help the parties translate what they have accepted as closely as possible into the terms of an agreement and in language which is clearly understood.

OBSERVER: I noticed another respect in which you demonstrated a distinct lack of shyness. Quite frankly, after the Employer's attorney raised concerns about the settlement on this issue, I was surprised by your degree of forcefulness both on the telephone with him and with the Employer committee after the telephone call. You told me the day before yesterday that "these negotiations belong to the parties." You certainly did not seem to be letting them call the shots.

MEDIATOR: That's absolutely right. In the beginning, I have an obligation to listen to both parties explain their views and feelings about the issues. After I have listened, however, I have to do something other than simply carry messages back and forth or there is no purpose to my being a part of the process. As I said before, I find it helpful to think of a mediator as a third participant in the negotiations. After listening to both sides, the mediator must form an impression as to what would constitute a possible basis for settlement that both sides could sell to their constituency. The mediator may have more than one possibility in mind, but, at a minimum, the mediator should have at least some impression in mind as to what would constitute a possible basis for settlement.

OBSERVER: How does your role change once you have that impression in mind?

The mediator is a third negotiator, representing a possible basis for settlement

<19>

MEDIATOR: Once that impression has been developed, the mediator then becomes, as I have said, a negotiator who is advancing that basis for settlement to both parties. When I develop an impression as to what I believe would be an appropriate basis for settling a particular issue, I don't hesitate in the least to try to persuade both parties that they should agree along those lines.

OBSERVER: What do you mean by an appropriate basis for settlement. What makes it appropriate?

MEDIATOR: When I use that word, I'm talking about what's salable: the settlement I have a realistic chance of persuading both sides to accept. Some mediators talk about facilitating a fair settlement, but I don't think that's a good term to use. Everyone has a different notion of what is fair. That is a standard that is personal to each individual, and I am *not* imposing my personal standards on the parties. My goal is identifying a salable solution and then working for its adoption.

OBSERVER: That sounds good, but how do you know in advance what will be salable? Let's work with a concrete example. You decided that the percentage in the formula for the supplemental benefit would have to be much closer to the Employer's opening offer of 50% than the Union's first offer of 100%. What made you decide that the salable solution was in that range?

MEDIATOR: The parties. Everything they said and did affected my impression. The way the Employer talked about the percentage was important, and the positions it took were important. The Employer showed movement on every aspect of the issue *except* the percentage. It took creativity and finesse to get them up to 60%.

OBSERVER: It sounds like a party will do better with you if they "play hardball," and stick to one position. Aren't you saying that will cause you to push for a settlement that is close to the hard line that has been adopted?

MEDIATOR: You haven't got the full picture. There's another part of my job that becomes very important here. Parties to a mediation frequently display a tough stance that is far from the bottom line because they think what you call "hardball" tactics will produce a deal more favorable to them. They run a substantial risk, of course, that there will be *no* deal at all. When I believe this is happening, it's my job to cause that party to be more realistic.

OBSERVER: How do you do that?

MEDIATOR: This is where the "pressure points" come in. I remind them of the alternative they face if there is no deal. Here it's a strike. The Employer has to decide how big a pill that would be for it to swallow. At times, I have to remind the Employer that it may wish to swallow some smaller pills in order to avoid that big pill. I did that at the end of the session today when I was trying to persuade the Employer about the language committing them to discuss retiree benefits in the future.

OBSERVER: Is there any other way you can talk a party into dropping a hard line?

MEDIATOR: Yes. I said before that everyone has their own idea of fairness. Some things, however, are less open to question than others. If a party is taking a position that almost anyone would call unfair, there's a good chance it will destroy the mediation. The other side may give up on the process and call things off. Since it's my job to keep things moving positively, I try to avoid this result by talking parties out of any positions that could lead to proper outrage. I did that today when the Employer wanted to pull benefits for retirees that it had previously offered off the table. I told the Employer that in my judgment that position would cause a blow-up.

OBSERVER: Doesn't that mean that your personal judgments have played a part in shaping the settlement? Is it proper for a mediator who is an outsider to the dispute to affect the positions of the parties in that manner?

MEDIATOR: I don't make any bones about that. The parties have the full benefit of my judgments and experience. They asked me to mediate this dispute. I didn't stick my nose in uninvited. So far as I'm concerned, that means that they wanted me to bring my experience to bear in helping them settle issues where they are at a standstill.

OBSERVER: Why do you think you succeeded in

prodding the Employer committee to agree despite their attorney's cautionary advice?

MEDIATOR: At that stage, we had accomplished a great deal in a comparatively short period of time. The Union identified the topic of pensions as the most critical issue in the negotiations. The parties were stymied on that issue before the mediation began. In one afternoon, I was able to bring both parties very, very close together so that only one or two minor points remained to be resolved. That gave both sides tremendous confidence in the mediation process. It was accomplishing significant things that they had not been able to accomplish for themselves. I think it was that confidence in the mediation process that made the Employer committee receptive to my recommendation.

OBSERVER: I noticed at other times you were very careful to let one or the other side know when you had worked very hard to get a particular concession. At least once you made things appear tougher than they really had been. Did you have a purpose in mind?

MEDIATOR: Yes I did. My primary purpose fits in with the observation that I just made. Progress in mediation spawns more progress because it makes both sides more willing to make concessions, rather than withholding possible changes in position. Therefore, when I feel that my efforts have produced significant results, I let the other side know that the progress is substantial. I'm not doing that to toot my own horn. I'm doing that to let them know that there is cause to have confidence in the mediation process.

OBSERVER: Well, I think I have some sense as to why the effort this afternoon was as successful as it turned out to be. Do you think the discussion tonight regarding wages can possibly be as successful?

MEDIATOR: There's no way to know.

Joint Session 8:30 P.M.

MEDIATOR: My notes from our first meeting indicate that the Union's last proposal on wages called for guarantees of $30,000 in the first year, $34,000 in the second year, and $38,000 in the third year. The Opera's last proposal called for no money guarantees, but, as I recall, you agreed to develop some language we could use as a basis for discussion.

EMPLOYER REPRESENTATIVE: I sure didn't agree to discuss anything like $38,000. If they're going to talk in those terms there's no point in bickering about language. In any language, that's ridiculous. We've shown everyone here our financial statement. We're not hiding bags of money, you know.

MEDIATOR: Well, let's be candid on this subject. Without reference to the numbers themselves, it is clear to me that we may not be able to reach an agreement unless there is some guarantee of some sort. The fact seems to be that the Opera has populated the orchestra with a large number of younger players. These persons, as the Union has pointed out to us, need to have some assurance of a guaranteed salary since they are in the process of raising families and buying homes. They are seeking a certain stability of income. Now can't you describe your economic proposal in a way that gives them *some* bottom line figure that they can count on? We don't have to talk about what that figure will be right now. Let's try to agree on a concept that will give the musicians that kind of bottom line figure.

EMPLOYER REPRESENTATIVE: Well, we have considered the Union's approach and while we are very reluctant to even consider the matter of a guarantee, we do have a suggestion along these lines that we have worked up. We developed it after our first meeting, and if there is to be any guarantee, it will have to be within this framework.

This proposal includes three basic parts. First, it continues the *time* guarantees included in the current agreement, namely, 20 weeks of employment during the regular season, 12 preliminary days, and 80 rehearsal hours. Secondly, as requested by the Union, it sets forth that each and every member of the orchestra will be guaranteed an annual income *greater than* the amount paid for the time guaranteed. Now that's what the Union has been asking for. To accomplish this, however, there has to be a third part to the plan which the Union has *not* discussed.

MEDIATOR: What's that?

EMPLOYER REPRESENTATIVE: Thirdly, and most importantly so far as we are concerned, the proposal lists various outside jobs generated by the Opera which will count towards satisfaction of the new money guarantee. You will see the proposed language indicates that should a musician decline any of these outside jobs that are offered, the amount that would have been earned will be deducted from the guarantee.

We have worked very hard on this proposal and we believe it should be satisfactory to both sides. It enables us to include a dollar figure in the agreement that more closely reflects what musicians are actually earning. At the same time, it affords the Opera some protection against what has been of concern to us. The Union's past proposals haven't said anything about what work counts against the guarantee, or what happens when a musician turns down work. Obviously, we do not want to pay out money without receiving income-generating services. We think the list of extra work generated by the Opera should adequately protect us against that problem. Here is our proposal in writing (shown below).

Employer Proposal
Day Number 3/8:30 P.M.

I. Employment Guarantee
   1. Employer guarantees that each performance year shall consist of not less than twenty (20) weeks of six services at Opera contract rates (the "guaranteed weeks"). In addition, the Employer guarantees four daytime rehearsal hours for each performance week, cumulatively applied; and 12 paid days of preliminary rehearsal during each performance year.
   2. Minimum guarantee at Opera proposed rates = $19,154.00.

II. Minimum Compensation Guarantee
   1. Employer guarantees the following minimum compensation to each member of the 69 member orchestra:

Year 1 _____
Year 2 _____
Year 3 _____
Year 4 _____

2. All compensation generated by the Opera and its Affiliates, at appropriate rates, shall be counted towards the minimum compensation guarantee. This includes, but is not limited to, the following:
   a. Summer and Fall seasons;
   b. Tours;
   c. Concerts;
   d. Ballet;
   e. Student/Senior matinees;
   f. Special programs;
   g. Vacation pay, seniority pay, etc.;
   h. Media compensation (radio, television, recording, etc.);
   i. Any employment generated by the Opera.
3. Credit for Refused Employment: When optional employment is offered to a Player, and said Player refuses such offer of employment, then Opera may credit the actual amount that said player would have earned for the engagement against the Minimum Compensation Guarantee.

> MEDIATOR: (Speaking to the Union committee) Obviously, you're going to need some time to review this. Do you have any preliminary questions you want to raise now before caucusing?
>
> UNION REPRESENTATIVE: No, but we may have some questions once we begin discussing it. We'll let you know.

Further Developments: A lengthy Union caucus followed. No questions were relayed during that time. At approximately 10:30 P.M., the Union representative requested a further joint session.

Joint Session 10:30 P.M.

> UNION REPRESENTATIVE: We've gone over this in some detail and we think the Employer's proposal may set forth a concept that will accomplish our goals. We'll have to work with the list of jobs outside the Opera itself counting against the money guarantee, however. We simply don't think that inclusion of some of these

A CASE STUDY   65

jobs is appropriate. (The Union representative then highlighted special programs, matinees, and seniority pay as three items which the Union urged should be excluded.)

EMPLOYER REPRESENTATIVE: If you're going to start picking this list apart, then the two of us are not talking about the same concept. These are all outside jobs which the Opera generates. And we're not going to agree to any form of money guarantee unless all work the Opera generates is counted against that money guarantee. If it's not set up that way, then there's too great a danger we'll end up paying out money for nothing. There's no justification for that, and we're not even going to talk about a structure that could lead to that.

UNION REPRESENTATIVE: Well, we may be at a logjam then, because we simply don't see any chance that our membership would accept this form of guarantee.

MEDIATOR: What precisely is the problem?

> Expose specific problems that are behind positions
>
> <11>

UNION REPRESENTATIVE: Let me explain what the problem is. Including things like "special programs" has some consequences that aren't obvious. In recent years, the Opera has created one or two large-scale extra jobs that have used about two-thirds of the orchestra. From all we hear, it looks like those jobs will continue. The way this thing is set up, the Opera has a great incentive to spread work around, so that no one has to be paid off at the end of the year. That means that the one third of the musicians who were not involved in a large-scale extra job would be offered a complete hodgepodge of different kinds of work at odd times. They would have a great deal of difficulty planning any sort of regular schedule for themselves, and if they turned down any of this work, that would be deducted from their money guarantee. It simply looks to us as though this would create a heck of a lot of dissension and unhappiness. We've talked about it among ourselves, and we simply don't think the membership would go for this.

EMPLOYER REPRESENTATIVE: The only way we can

even discuss a money guarantee is along the lines we have suggested. *All* work generated by the Opera must count against the money guarantee. And we're certainly not going to pay people who turn down work. It can't be talked about otherwise.

UNION REPRESENTATIVE: Then I guess it can't be talked about because we don't see any chance of this flying.

Try another approach if a roadblock is encountered

<9>

MEDIATOR: Well, perhaps it would be best to put this aside and try to reach an economic settlement on the weekly base rate and other figures, without using an annual salary guarantee. We can always come back to this at a later time if someone has new ideas to offer. Let's meet tomorrow morning at 10 o'clock and see if we can't make some progress on the weekly base rate.

Summary of Events
(Day Number 3; Second Session)

After the parties' economic positions were first discussed on Day 1, the Mediator evaluated the differences between the parties and the elements critical to each party for settlement. He concluded that the Union was committed to securing new contract language that would give its members a bottom-line earnings figure they could rely upon. He also concluded that the Opera's financial posture would preclude it from agreeing to any guaranteed payments unless they could be fairly certain that nothing would be owed to most musicians at the end of the year beyond compensation for services performed.

In this session, the Mediator actively guided the parties toward discussion of a concept capable of giving *both* the ingredients they found necessary. The Mediator encouraged the Opera to develop language that would satisfy the Union's expressed need for a bottom-line figure representing earnings that could be relied upon.

When discussion of that language evidenced that agreement was not currently possible, he suggested a different approach for attempting resolution of economic issues, namely, negotiation regarding base rates for performance weeks, preliminary days, and rehearsal hours. He hoped to keep things progressing while both sides continued to reassess the guarantee concept. This prevented either side from becoming unnecessarily locked into an immobile position.

The results of the session were discussed in the following conversation:

Private Conversation 11:30 P.M.

OBSERVER: I was rather surprised to see the Employer's guarantee proposal bite the dust so early. It did seem to address concerns we heard both sides raise in our first preliminary meeting. The Union has been after a simple statement of a financial guarantee that could be readily understood by a loan officer or anyone else. That was part of the proposal. And it seemed to give the Employer the protection against paying out money when no work has been performed, which it has been insisting upon.

Consider whether problems are as big as the parties suggest
<11>

MEDIATOR: Don't be so sure we've seen the last of that concept. The Union and Employer guarantee proposals really have only one difference in concept. Think carefully about the objection the Union raised. They don't want musicians to be forced into taking a lot of odd jobs. Only one feature of the Employer proposal would cause that, namely, the proviso requiring a *reduction* in the guarantee if anyone turns down a job. That means counting extra earnings against the guarantee should not be a problem for the Union; it just doesn't want musicians to lose some of the guarantee if they turn down work from the Opera. The Employer's approach may look a lot more attractive to the Union after it finds out what can be accomplished by dickering with the base wage rates. The Employer may also become more willing to modify the concept as time progresses and the strike deadline approaches. I plan to keep this guarantee alternative in mind, because it may well become useful before we're done.

Keep options in mind, even if temporarily unsatisfactory to one party
<9>

The Mediator really has the responsibility of always keeping in mind the entire agreement and what occurred with reference to rejected proposals. He may be able to use them later, or he may simply be required to dispose of them in order to finalize a complete settlement. Either way, they can't be forgotten.

Putting it another way, the Mediator must have a

game plan in mind and always should be in a position to reintroduce a "play" into the plan which at a particular time failed to make a "gain," using the parlance of football. The play may work the second time or the third time.

Day Number 4

Joint Session 10:00 A.M.

MEDIATOR: Both sides have proposals outstanding as to what the base rates should be for performance weeks, preliminary days, rehearsal hours, and outside jobs. In light of our discussion last evening, I think it would be most productive if we make a real effort to reach agreement on those items. If we are successful, we may not need to further discuss the notion of a guarantee. If we're not, we can always pursue the concept of a guarantee at a later time.

(Speaking to the Union representative) I'm going to ask your group to caucus and see if you can't come up with a new comprehensive proposal on the economics. Include your position on vacations, as well, because I see from the documents you've given me there's an outstanding dispute on that issue. Do you think your group can accomplish that?

UNION REPRESENTATIVE: We'll put together the best proposal we can.

Further Developments: The Union representative brought a three-page proposal to the Mediator two hours later at approximately noon. Each page set forth proposed economic terms for one year of a three-year agreement. From this point forward, all of the Union's economic proposals were based on a three-year agreement even though the pension settlement presumed a four-year agreement. The Employer's proposals continued to be based on a four-year agreement.

The economic terms proposed by the Union at this stage included weekly base rates, preliminary day rates, and extra rehearsal hour rates. It specified that *all* musicians would be guaranteed 15 extra days of work for the Ballet. Beyond this, however, it did not contain any guarantees. It did forecast how much most musicians could count on from extra work.

Throughout the three years, the day and hour rates remained a constant fraction of the proposed weekly rate. Since all rates were derived from the weekly base rate for guaranteed performance weeks, *only that weekly base rate will be discussed from this point forward in the Case Study.* The Union's proposal is set forth below. The Mediator promptly provided the Employer committee with a copy of this proposal and invited them to study and respond. Little more was said at that time.

Union Proposal
Day Number 4/10:00 A.M.

I. Year 1

   1. *Time Guarantees/Base Rates*

20 performance weeks @ $815 =	16,300
3 preliminary weeks @ $815 =	2,445
100 rehearsal hours @ 27.50 =	2,750
	21,495

   2. *Vacation*

3 weeks @ $815 =	2,445
	23,940

   3. *Seniority Pay*
      Current System with

1 week minimum @ $815 =	815
	24,755

   4. *Guaranteed Work*

Ballet—15 days @ reg. rates =	2,445
	27,200

   5. *Expected Extra Earnings*

Special Program, OT, etc. =	2,300
Year 1	29,500

II. Year 2

   1.

20 performance weeks @ $895 =	17,900
3 preliminary weeks @ $895 =	2,685
100 rehearsal hours @ $ 30.25 =	3,025
	23,610

2. *Vacation*
   4 weeks @ $895 =   3,580
                                                      ──────
                                                      27,190

3. *Seniority Pay*
   Current System with
   1 week minimum @ $895 =   895
                                                      ──────
                                                      28,085

4. *Guaranteed Work*
   Ballet—15 days @ reg. rates =   2,685
                                                      ──────
                                                      30,770

5. *Expected Extra Earnings*
   Special Programs, OT, etc. =   2,300
                                                      ──────
                         Year 2   33,070

III. Year 3

1. *Time Guarantees/Base Rates*
   20 performance weeks @ $985 =   19,700
     3 preliminary weeks @ $985 =   2,955
   100 rehearsal hours @ $ 33.25 =   3,325
                                                      ──────
                                                      25,980

2. *Vacation*
   5 weeks @ $985 =   4,925
                                                      ──────
                                                      30,905

3. *Seniority Pay*
   Current System with
   1 week minimum @ $985 =   985
                                                      ──────
                                                      31,890

4. *Guaranteed Work*
   Ballet—15 days @ reg. rates =   2,955
                                                      ──────
                                                      34,845

5. *Expected Extra Earnings*
   Special Programs, OT, etc. =   2,300
                         Year 3   37,145

Private Conversation 12:30 P.M.

OBSERVER: What are you doing?

MEDIATOR: I'm comparing this to the proposals the

Union had outstanding before the mediation began. I want to see how much movement they have made.

OBSERVER: Why don't you simply wait to see how the Employer group reacts to the wage proposal? That should make pretty clear whether we are progressing.

Know the facts
<12>

MEDIATOR: I mentioned before that it is very important for the mediator to understand the facts just as well, if not better, than the parties. If progress has been made, I want to be able to highlight that progress when I speak to the Employer committee.

OBSERVER: Well, how does the proposal look?

MEDIATOR: The Union has taken a very interesting approach. They have made phenomenal movement on the weekly base rate, particularly in the first year of the agreement. Before the mediation, the Union was proposing $965/$1060/$1165 per week for a three-year agreement. The proposal now is for $815/$895/$985 per week. But the Union has fattened up other parts of the economic package in order to reach a bottom line very similar to what was on the table before mediation. The time guarantees are improved. The old contract has 20 performance weeks, 12 preliminary days, and 80 rehearsal hours. This proposal bumps the preliminary days to 3 weeks (or 15 days) and the rehearsal hours to 100. That gives them more money.

The Union picks up much more under their vacation proposal. According to the documents I reviewed during Day 2, the Opera's vacation plan has really been a form of seniority pay. Employees have received a percentage of their earnings for the 20 performance weeks, which is determined according to length of service. This has been great for long-time employees and lousy for new employees. For the first year, this document proposes three weeks of vacation for every musician, *and* continuation of the seniority pay plan, with a one-week minimum. That amounts to a minimum of four weeks paid vacation for everyone.

As a result of these factors, the minimum annual

earnings resulting from these proposals would be approximately $29,500/$33,000/$37,000 over the life of the agreement. That's only slightly less than the guarantees the Union proposed before mediation.

OBSERVER: What strategy do you think is behind this?

Determine what each party needs to settle
<19>

MEDIATOR: I would say they are trying to entice the Employer committee with substantial movement on the weekly base rate for the first year of the agreement, while hoping to pick up some gains in other areas. I don't know how the Employer will react, but I do have one thought at this stage. That $30,000 plateau has a lot of significance to the Union. Their representative mentioned that figure in our very first meeting when he spoke of the need for a guarantee. And you can see that they worked with the figures in this proposal to keep the minimum earnings resulting in the first year as close as possible to $30,000. I don't see any sign that this thing could be settled for $30,000 in the first year, but my current judgment is that reaching this figure sometime during the term of the agreement may be vital to reaching a settlement.

OBSERVER: What could possibly be so magical about that figure, as opposed to $29,000 or $31,000?

MEDIATOR: Very frequently in the course of a mediation, the behavior of one party suggests to me that a particular figure has taken on "magical" significance so far as they are concerned. Discussions leading up to the negotiations or other factors have instilled that figure as a goal. And that party needs to attain that goal in order to feel successful and sell the resulting package enthusiastically to those whose approval may be necessary. In my experience, there are unquestionably times when $29,999.99 will not settle a deal but $30,000 will. My opinion may change, but right now it looks to me as though that figure has significance.

Further Developments: At this point, the Employer's primary representative entered the room where the Mediator and Observer were speaking.

EMPLOYER REPRESENTATIVE: This is absolutely ridiculous. I don't see any point in what we're doing. If this is all that they can accomplish, we might just as well go back to the office and send back everyone's season tickets.

MEDIATOR: Calm down. What's the problem?

EMPLOYER REPRESENTATIVE: We've been knocking our brains out here, and they haven't made any movement whatsoever. That $815 figure looks fine. But when you take this thing apart, it's the fattest package they've had on the table. They're proposing a minimum of four weeks vacation for every single musician, and we don't even offer full-time employment. A two-week minimum might be worth talking about, but four weeks is ridiculous. And these increased time guarantees are totally unrealistic.

Direct the parties to topics where progress is possible

<9>

MEDIATOR: I'm going to borrow from a colleague of mine in China. The other evening I was watching a program about mediation of family disputes in China. The Chinese mediator said something that definitely applies here, "You can't eat a hot bun in one bite." These negotiations have been bogged down for months, and we knew that one proposal was not going to bridge the difference on each and every issue. Concentrate on the issues where they have made considerable movement. You like what they've done on the weekly base rate for the first year, so let's see what we can do with that issue. Give me a meaningful counterproposal to the $815, and do whatever you need to on the other issues.

EMPLOYER REPRESENTATIVE: All right, but this does not give me much cause for hope.

MEDIATOR: Concentrate on the issues that do give you cause for hope. The weekly base rate in the first year of the agreement is clearly one; and see if you can't inspire some significant movement on other fronts.

Further Developments: After this conversation, the Mediator shuttled three economic counterproposals between the parties. They contained the following proposed weekly base rates:

2:30 P.M. Employer Proposal:
Year: 1   /   2   /   3   /   4
          $785 / $825 / $865 / $905   per week

3:10 P.M. Union Proposal:
Abandoned approach of making gains through substantial improvement in time guarantees and vacations; addressed Year 1 only: $965.

3:30 P.M. Employer Proposal:
Year: 1   /   2   /   3   /   4
          $795 / $835 / $875 / $915   per week
($10 above last proposal in all years.)

When the last proposal was presented to the Union committee the Union representative looked at it quickly, after which the following conversation took place:

Conversation with Union Committee 3:40 P.M.

UNION REPRESENTATIVE: Look, I can see what they have done here and as far as we're concerned it's not much. We've spent the entire day making headway by nickels and dimes. It's a farce even to pretend that this could lead to a settlement, and they should know that. We don't see any point in staying here today. We have a meeting of the membership scheduled for tomorrow, and we want to take some time to prepare for that. We would like to have a joint session to make clear to them the futility of what they're doing, and then we'll have to call it quits for the day.

Further Developments: A joint session was convened in order to allow the Union to state its position. In light of the Union membership meeting scheduled to take place on Day 5, mediation was scheduled to continue at 9:00 A.M. on Day 6.

Summary of Events
(Day Number 4)

During Day 4, the parties began to work on very specific economic issues (the base rates and vacation pay) for the first time in the Mediation. Because this was the first time that the parties worked specifically on base rates and vacation pay, the Mediator took time to size up the situation, just as he did at the early stages of the pension and retiree benefits discussion. He carefully analyzed the nature of the position changes made by each party in order to begin forming some impression about what might be a salable settlement. This careful analysis enabled him to point out progress to the Employer group and produce a constructive counterproposal from them at a time when they were quite discouraged.

The next Union proposal seemed to take a radically different tack. It actually moved *away* from agreement on the first-year base rate. Even though the Union responded with a *non*productive proposal that put the parties further apart on the first-year base rate, the Mediator did *not* try to talk them out of it. It wasn't the right time to take such an activist approach, for reasons explained in the following conversation:

Private Conversation 4:30 P.M.

OBSERVER: Why did you let things break up today without putting up a fight? On Day 3, you kept them working at a breakneck pace until late into the evening.

MEDIATOR: I mentioned to you before that sometimes there simply is no substitute for the passage of time in negotiation. The proposal the Union made at 3:10 P.M. made clear that the Union is simply not prepared today to make the movement necessary in order to settle these issues. In that proposal, they returned to the weekly base rate they were proposing before mediation began. I'll tell you how I size things up. The Union committee members are probably a little bit wary of moving too far too quickly for a couple of reasons. First, the deadline we are up against is a full week from now. I understand that in the past these parties have always negotiated up until the eleventh hour. They may think more will be gained if the pressure is kept on a little longer. More important, I sense from some of the side conversations I have had that they don't want to move further without being certain that they have their membership's support. That's why the Union has scheduled a meeting of all the musicians. It's too early to vote on anything, but the committee will be making a report. Negotiations are a learning process, and the membership, who will be called upon to approve any agreement, must be made a part of that process. I am sure the committee members are hesitant to move just before this meeting, without testing the water to find out whether what's been accomplished so far will be accepted by the membership. If the pension/retirement settlement goes over well in that meeting, that could well have a positive impact when we resume day after tomorrow.

Day Number 6

Further Developments: Day 6 began at 9:00 A.M. with a joint session. At that joint session, the Mediator invited the Union committee to prepare a comprehensive economic proposal, in light of whatever it may have learned at its membership meeting. The Mediator called attention to the fact that the last comprehensive proposal made had come from the Employer. After the Union committee worked for 2½ hours, the Union representative presented the Mediator with a proposal for the first year of an agreement. It proposed a weekly base rate of *$810* and continuation of the existing seniority pay for vacation, with a minimum of two weeks' pay.

This vacation proposal brought the parties into the same ball park. The Employer had already shown some receptiveness to a two-week minimum vacation benefit. Although counterproposals on this issue were exchanged throughout negotiations on economic issues, they will be excluded from the Case Study until Day 10 because they assumed lesser significance.

This one-year economic proposal was passed on to the Employer committee which, at approximately 1:15 P.M., produced a counterproposal with the following base rates: $795/$835/$875/$915 per week. That led to the following discussion:

> MEDIATOR: I told you at the beginning that I do not possess a particular magic, but I do have quite a few years of experience. I assume you had that in mind when you selected me for this job.
>
> EMPLOYER REPRESENTATIVE: Yes.

A Case Study   77

Uncover possible movement, and <18>

Direct its use with careful timing <21>

MEDIATOR: Well, in light of that experience, I want to make a suggestion to you. When we broke off in the afternoon of Day 4, you had $795 on the table for the weekly base rate in the first year of the agreement. There's been a lot of gnashing of teeth since that time. The Union spent quite a lot of time this morning bringing themselves to the point of proposing $810. I think we are at a critical stage, and I think they need to see some positive feedback. Obviously, you have to decide what you can afford to propose. But let me simply suggest this. If you have a card which you have been holding to play at a key moment, this is it. If you have authorization to improve that first year figure, I would suggest that this is the time to do it.

EMPLOYER REPRESENTATIVE: Well, we can go to $800 in the first year, but we thought this might be a little early to have that out on the table.

MEDIATOR: You might as well up your offer to $800 because I'll tell you right now that nothing less than that is going to fly. As I said before, their committee agonized in coming down to $810, and I don't think they can move any further unless they get some positive feedback. Let me just ask you to think this over. I'm not going to pass anything to them until you discuss it and get back to me. You might give thought to another item as well. The idea of a money guarantee was shelved. Their ideas may have changed, however, as a result of the membership meeting. You might give thought to including some supplemental guarantee for income to be produced by Opera-generated extra jobs in this proposal. I would say this is a good time to find out whether that can be of any help in putting together a mutually agreeable package.

EMPLOYER REPRESENTATIVE: All right, we'll look at the figures further.

Further Developments: The Employer presented the Mediator with a revised proposal at 3:00 P.M. It adopted the Mediator's recommendation to move up to $800 in the first year. Its other terms were as follows:

3:00 P.M. Employer Proposal:
    $800 / $835 / $875 / $915 per week
Supplemental Guarantee
    $1,500 / $1,600 / $1,700 / $1,800 per year

The following conversation took place between the Mediator and the Employer representative regarding this proposal:

MEDIATOR: I want to make sure that I understand the Supplemental Guarantee you have in mind before I present it to them. How will this work?

EMPLOYER REPRESENTATIVE: This is the same concept we had on the table before. All extra income the Opera generates counts toward satisfying this guarantee.

MEDIATOR: What do you mean by "extra?"

EMPLOYER REPRESENTATIVE: All the work we generate above and beyond the time guarantees we agree to. Right now, that's 20 weeks, 12 preliminary days, and 80 rehearsal hours.

MEDIATOR: So you are offering a type of guarantee beyond what's in the old contract?

EMPLOYER REPRESENTATIVE: Absolutely. This says that in the first year of the new agreement they can all count on $1500 more than the time guarantees generate.

MEDIATOR: I'll see what I can do with this.

Further Developments: When the Mediator presented this proposal to the Union committee, the following conversation took place:

UNION REPRESENTATIVE: 800 bucks! Couldn't they come up to the $810 we proposed? We came down far lower than we ever intended too, you know.

Be firm when there is no more to be gained by dickering

<19>

MEDIATOR: I worked very hard to get that $800 for you and I can tell you with certainty that there's no more there. I cleaned their pockets and this is an issue we ought to wrap up. That's only $10 less than you were proposing, you know.

UNION REPRESENTATIVE: All right, we'll look at the $800. Now what's this guarantee about? Is that the same thing they were talking about before? If a musician turns down work, will there be an offset?

A Case Study   79

MEDIATOR: Yes, it's the same concept, but they've added figures to the picture.

UNION REPRESENTATIVE: Well, these figures aren't going to get them anywhere.

MEDIATOR: Look, I don't expect things to settle at these figures, but you've got some money there that wasn't on the table before. They're telling you that each and every musician may count on making $1,500 more than the time guarantees produce in the first year of the agreement. Take some time to see how that changes the picture and let me know what you can come back with.

Further Developments: After caucusing, the Union gave the Mediator a new proposal, and several counterproposals resulted, which were exchanged between the parties by the Mediator. The weekly base rate and supplemental guarantees contained in those proposals are summarized below with brief explanations in parentheses highlighting the movement made.

4:50 P.M. Union Proposal:
$800 / $900 / $1000 per week

Supplemental Guarantee
$1,750 / $2,250 / $2,750 per year

Authors' Comment: It should be observed that the Mediator's persuasion produced Union acceptance of the $800 base rate for the first year of the agreement and a Union counterproposal regarding the guarantee figures.

7:10 P.M. Employer Proposal:

$800 / $845 / $885 / $925 per week

(2nd, 3d & 4th years $10 greater)

Supplemental Guarantee

$1,600 / $1,600 / $1,700 / $1,800 per year

(1st year $100 greater)

9:10 P.M. Union Proposal:

$800 / $895 / $985 per week

(2nd year down $5; 3rd year down $15)

Supplemental Guarantee

$1,600 / $2,250 / $2,750 per year

(1st year down $150 from $1,750 to $1,600, producing *agreement* on that item)

12:10 A.M. Employer Proposal:

$800 / $850 / $900 per week

(2nd year up $5; 3rd year up $15)

Supplemental Guarantee

$1,600 / $1,700 / $1,800 per year

(2nd & 3rd years $100 greater)

Up to this point, the Employer's proposals all called for a four-year agreement (consistent with the settlement of issues affecting retirees) and the Union's proposals called for a three-year agreement. Upon making this proposal, the Employer shifted to a three-year agreement, without explanation.

1:10 A.M. Union Proposal:

$800 / $885 / $975 per week

(2nd & 3rd years down $10)

Supplemental Guarantee

$1,600 / $2,000 / $2,500 per year

(2nd & 3rd years down $250)

This proposal showed that the Union expected it to generate the following minimum annual salaries: $24,000/$27,000/$30,000. These figures were generated by adding the earnings that would result from guaranteed time, minimum vacation, and the supplemental guarantee.

Both parties described their last proposals above to the Mediator as the absolute best positions they were capable of putting on the table. This left the following gaps to be bridged: 1) *weekly base rate*: $35 in the 2nd year/$75 in the 3rd year; 2) *supplemental guarantee*: $300 in the 2nd year/$700 in the 3rd year. First year economics were essentially agreed upon, but neither party was willing to make any further movement on the terms for the second and third years. The Mediator called for a joint session.

Joint Session 1:30 A.M.

MEDIATOR: I'm not going to make any big speeches because I know you are all rather exhausted at this point, but I do want to make one observation and one suggestion. I want to commend all of you for the work that you have done thus far. We have agreement on the weekly base rate for the first year of the agreement and supplemental guarantee for the first year of the agreement. So far as I am concerned, that is the heart and soul of the economic package. I can tell you right now that the rest of the economic issues can come together and will come together before we are done. Your conduct thus far demonstrates to me that everyone here wants to reach an agreement and we are all now in the same ball park.

In my estimation, however, we may have accomplished as much regarding the economic package as we can accomplish at this stage. We also have numerous noneconomic issues that have to be resolved before Day 13. I'm going to suggest we take two days to tackle those noneconomic issues. That should leave us with sufficient time to return to the economic package. If we can finalize everything else, then that ought to fall into place as well.

I understand that the Employer committee members have to be involved in other meetings tomorrow afternoon. In light of the time, I suggest it would be best to plan on an evening meeting tomorrow, beginning at 7:00 P.M. That will give both sides a chance to review their priorities concerning the noneconomic issues.

(Speaking to the Union representative) According to my recollection, most of those originate from Union proposals. I would like your group to review those issues before tomorrow evening and see if you can't develop a list of your highest priorities. I'd like to take those up first.

UNION REPRESENTATIVE: All right. We are prepared to proceed in that fashion.

EMPLOYER REPRESENTATIVE: That sounds good to us.

Summary of Events
(Day Number 6)

The Mediator used the information he gathered on Day 4 to begin forming his own opinion about the shape of a salable settlement on the economic issues. During Day 6, he began very actively persuading both committees to move toward that settlement.

The Mediator began with a joint session in which he encouraged the Union to prepare a new comprehensive economic proposal. The Union committee took two and one-half hours to accomplish this. When it responded, its proposal included a beginning weekly base rate of $810, which was considerably closer to the Opera's outstanding proposal of $795 than the $965 that the Union had on the table before its membership meeting.

The Employer gave the Mediator a responsive proposal that stuck to the Opera's prior $795 position. The Mediator did *not* pass this proposal on to the Union. Rather, he encouraged the Opera to better its offer to $800 because he believed movement to that figure *then* was essential to settle the base rate for the first year. He also suggested reintroducing the concept of a supplemental guarantee. His encouragement was successful and the improved offer was passed on to the Union. At this point, the Mediator actively sought to persuade the Union to settle at the $800 figure and reconsider the guarantee concept. These efforts produced an exchange of proposals that brought the parties much closer together.

By 1:30 A.M., both sides appeared to be at the end of the line and there was still some distance between them. The Mediator did not "strong-arm" either side at this point. The Mediator concluded, for reasons explained in the following conversation, that neither side would be likely to move further on money until closer to the Day 13 deadline. Both would be likely to fear that movement now would only be followed by pressure for more movement later, and, therefore, would be likely to "sit" on any "cushion" left.

For these reasons, the Mediator shifted efforts to the numerous noneconomic issues left to be resolved, all of which also needed to be dealt with before Day 13. This maintained positive momentum and avoided frustration by either or both parties over the lack of a full economic settlement.

These developments were discussed in the following conversation:

A CASE STUDY 83

Private Conversation 2:00 A.M.

OBSERVER: I wasn't sure what you would do when both sides said they had gone as far as possible. What was your thinking?

Be sensitive to timing
<21>

MEDIATOR: I said it before and I will say it again—sometimes there simply is no substitute for the passage of time in negotiation, and mediation, as we have discussed, is a form of negotiation. We have overcome the most difficult hurdles on the economic front. The first year of the agreement is nearly finalized. But it appears clear to me that neither party is going to be able to move that last yard until they are closer to the strike deadline. They both want to wait for the other guy to blink. In this circumstance, a change of topics is critical in order to prevent the parties from tiring and beginning to feel that no agreement is possible. I am hopeful that we can establish a positive tone by resolving the noneconomic issues so that both sides will be prepared to move half a yard when we get back to the economic package.

OBSERVER: Has your overview on the economic issues changed at all since this morning.

MEDIATOR: No, I'd say today's events confirm what I said earlier. The Union has clearly given up any thought of reaching that $30,000 plateau in the first year of the agreement. You will note, however, that their last proposal was crafted in such a way that minimum annual earnings of $30,000 could be expected in the last year of the agreement. That confirms my prior impression that the $30,000 plateau has a magic to it. I think the final economic package will have to recognize that in order to assure its salability.

OBSERVER: Well, I assume you'll be sleeping in tomorrow.

MEDIATOR: Not on your life. I want to review the outstanding noneconomic proposals in detail before the parties get here at 7:00 P.M.

Day Number 7

Private Conversation 3:30 P.M.

OBSERVER: How do you plan to proceed this evening when we take up the noneconomic issues?

MEDIATOR: I'm not sure, but I think it may be productive to work in joint meetings for a time.

OBSERVER: Why are you inclined toward that route? "Shuttle diplomacy" created some tremendous progress on economic issues.

MEDIATOR: Although the parties were in negotiations for a considerable period of time before the mediation began, I gather from several private conversations that their negotiations principally concerned the economic issues. I sense that the noneconomic issues have barely been discussed. In this circumstance, joint meetings may do a better job of flushing out information about the precise problems that have produced these proposals and alternate ways to address those problems.

OBSERVER: You've referred to these private conversations before. What exactly do you gain from them.

MEDIATOR: I'm sure you've noticed that while one committee is caucusing I very frequently chat with the members of the other committee. You may have thought I was just b-s-ing to fill the time, but I have a couple of purposes in mind when I do that. First, I am always reading the mood of participants in a negotiation. Are they optimistic or pessimistic? Do I need to emphasize what progress has been made to give them incentive? Are they concerned about concessions already made? All this helps me evaluate positions and plan my next move. This kind of information guides me in deciding whether to press for work around the clock or let up and allow a break. As I said before, it was private conversations that led me to conclude the Union group should not be pushed until after their membership meeting.

OBSERVER: I see what you mean. What's the second purpose you referred to?

MEDIATOR: Whenever it's appropriate during a mediation I inject stories about my experience. That tends to give the parties greater confidence in my recommendations. They know I'm not just guessing when I indicate what looks like an appropriate basis for settlement.

OBSERVER: How do you plan to begin the first joint meeting?

MEDIATOR: First, I will commend the parties for the progress we have made thus far. I know that we are close enough on the economic issues to put a package together before the Day 13 deadline, and they have worked very hard and conscientiously to bring that about. But there is a great deal of work yet to be done, and I want everyone to maintain a positive approach. Since most of the disputes on noneconomic issues result from Union proposals, I have asked the Union committee to produce a list of the noneconomic issues it regards as most important.

OBSERVER: Isn't that approach a little bit risky? If you reach a roadblock on one or two tough issues, might that not cause one side to break off the mediation? I would suspect that it would be easier to keep the parties at the table and easier to resolve one or two tough issues if all other matters have been settled and those one or two issues are all that stand between the parties and a successful opera season.

MEDIATOR: Sometimes I am guided by that kind of thinking. That is particularly true when the parties have made no progress whatsoever and there is a critical need to create some confidence that disputes can be settled and moves ought to be made. In that circumstance, I may well start with the items that can be most readily resolved. In this case, however, tremendous progress has been made. The parties have agreed on the concepts necessary to put together an economic settlement, and they have agreed on the weekly base rate for the first year of the agreement, as well as the supplemental guarantee for the first year of the agreement. I want to take advantage of this momentum and see if we can't resolve the noneconomic issues considered by the Union to be most crucial. If we succeed, that should induce the movement necessary to put together a final settlement on everything.

Further Developments: During the evening of Day 7 and throughout Days 8 and 9 the parties worked on the noneconomic issues. Principally, joint meetings followed by caucuses were used, although the Mediator did some shuttling between private committee meetings. The Union's first list of important economic issues contained 11 separate matters. Those were tackled first. Thereafter, the Union created a further list of less significant noneconomic issues and disputes with both economic and noneconomic consequences. Two examples of the issues identified as most important during this period have been selected for detailed presentation in this Case Study. Immediately following are the discussions that took place regarding those two issues.

Days Number 8 and 9

Joint Session Number 1

Further Developments: The following discussion took place as part of the first joint meeting over noneconomic issues. Preliminary comments about issues not treated in the Case Study have been omitted.

UNION REPRESENTATIVE: The next item I would like to discuss is the proposal of the musicians regarding conductors. Our proposal on this topic was as follows:

"Members of the orchestra and extras shall not be subject to any unprofessional abuse by any conductor, music director, personnel manager, or any other such person in a position to be in authority over the orchestra. (Examples of abuse: insults, false accusations, profanity, unjustified harassment.)

"If a musician, or group of musicians, feels such abuse has occurred, they may submit their complaint to the orchestra. The orchestra shall then take a vote as to whether or not the offending party shall be hired again by the Opera company. A majority vote shall determine if the offending party is to be reengaged."

Now, I need to be frank with you. This proposal has been identified by our membership as the most critical noneconomic issue. I don't think the Opera has taken this proposal seriously thus far, and they are going to have to take it seriously if we intend to reach a settlement.

EMPLOYER REPRESENTATIVE: How can we take seriously a proposal on your part to take over the Opera? That's precisely what you are suggesting. You are suggesting that the musicians should have the right to fire a conductor. If we were even to think about agreeing to such a thing, we would be fired! You had better explain to your members that there is simply no way the Opera is going to turn over management to the musicians.

MEDIATOR: I'm going to ask each of you to review your positions on this issue further during the next caucus. We have some other items where counterproposals are warranted, and the caucus will give you time to discuss any possible solutions you might be able to offer on this issue.

UNION REPRESENTATIVE: The next thing that we would like to discuss relates to a dispute that arose during the term of the last agreement. For the performance of one opera, the conductor decided not to have the principal, or first chair, in a particular section play the part that is normally played by the principal. We had to file a grievance which went all the way to arbitration.

EMPLOYER REPRESENTATIVE: So what's your problem? Didn't you get everything you wanted from the arbitration?

UNION REPRESENTATIVE: So far as we are concerned, it should be our mutual goal to avoid arbitrations. Negotiations are the time to address problems in a way that will prevent future arbitrations, not leave us in a position where future arbitrations are inevitable. We want to clean up this problem so it won't require grievances in the future.

MEDIATOR: What was the result of the arbitration?

UNION REPRESENTATIVE: Well, the arbitrator ruled that the Opera was required to pay the principal the same wages that would have been earned had the assignment not been changed.

EMPLOYER REPRESENTATIVE: In our opinion, it was an erroneous decision, but the amount of money involved did not warrant challenging it in court.

MEDIATOR: (Speaking to the Employer committee) I'm going to ask you to consider this entire matter during your caucus and determine whether you can't propose an addition to the contract that would address the Union's concern. Keep in mind that the arbitration award received during the term of the last contract is going to have some impact on what occurs in the future, unless specific language is added. If you keep that in mind, it might help you to come up with a proposal.

Further Developments: After completion of this joint meeting, both committees caucused. While they were doing so, the Mediator entered the room being used by the Employer committee, where the following conversation took place:

MEDIATOR: Have you had an opportunity to consider the issue concerning principal musicians yet?

EMPLOYER REPRESENTATIVE: I still don't see why we need to do anything. They won the arbitration. Why aren't they satisfied?

MEDIATOR: Because they don't want to spend money for needless arbitrations during the term of this agreement, and you shouldn't either. There's something you need to come to grips with here. If no change is made in the contract on this round, that award is going to be found highly persuasive when a case like it goes back to arbitration. It doesn't make much sense for both you and the Union to leave yourselves in a circumstance where money will have to be spent on that process.

EMPLOYER REPRESENTATIVE: We don't want to waste money on arbitrations, but if we put new language in, what are we going to get out of it? It shouldn't all go their way, you know?

Explain the consequences of positions taken by the parties
<13>

MEDIATOR: Keep in mind they have been urging that you have no right whatsoever to reassign principal musicians. If you offer a clause specifying that reassigned principals keep their usual contractual benefits, it will provide mutual recognition that you *can* make reassignments. That will give you something you didn't have before. And such a clause would prevent any future arbitrator from ordering you not to reassign principals.

EMPLOYER REPRESENTATIVE: That's not a bad point. Maybe your suggestion is better than arbitration. We'll talk about it among ourselves.

After both parties completed their private conferences, a further joint meeting occurred for the purpose of reporting the results of those caucuses.

Joint Session Number 2

Further Developments: As in the case of Joint Session Number 1, only the discussion regarding the two issues selected as examples follows.

EMPLOYER REPRESENTATIVE: In respect for the mediator's suggestion, we have reviewed your proposal regarding conductors carefully in our caucus session. But we could review this thing until the end of the earth, and our view would not change. So far as we are concerned, this proposal seeks to make the musicians the managers of the Opera.

UNION REPRESENTATIVE: Well, there will not be a settlement unless our concerns in this area are met.

Flush out specific problems that produced proposals
<11>

MEDIATOR: Let's talk about precisely what those concerns are. What exactly are the problems that have caused this proposal to be so important to the membership?

UNION REPRESENTATIVE: The proposal cites "insults, false accusations, profanity, and unjustified harassment" as examples of the kind of abuse it is designed to stop. That's exactly what, according to our members, has happened on occasion. It's not a problem with all of the conductors, but it has been a problem with at least one of the conductors. We simply feel his language is something to which our members should not be subjected.

MEDIATOR: Let me bring something into play here. When I was reviewing the expired contract in preparation for our first session, one provision in particular caught my eye. That is Article VI entitled "Working Conditions." Your contract reads, "Employer shall maintain safe, healthy and pleasant working conditions for all employees." That caught my eye because while many contracts guarantee safe and/or healthy working conditions, I have never seen one before that guaranteed "pleasant" working conditions. Now, I'm not your lawyer, and I can't give you advice about the legal meaning of the contract. But I can suggest that you ought to think about something. If I were in your shoes and felt that a particular conductor was abusing musicians with insults or profanity, I would file a grievance arguing that Article VI had been violated; I would argue that the Employer was not taking appropriate steps to assure "pleasant" working conditions. I think you ought to examine whether, perhaps, you already have the protection you are demanding. Perhaps this is not a problem that requires the addition of any new contract language. No one has proposed deleting Article VI from the agreement.

Authors' Comment: It should be recalled that the Mediator spent all of Day 2 reviewing the expiring agreement and the prior proposals of the parties. The comments above represent the "payoff" for that work. He was able to suggest a solution that had not occurred to either party.

EMPLOYER REPRESENTATIVE: I think you're moving a little quickly here. We're not admitting that any conductor we have hired harassed anyone in the past. We don't know whether that happened or not. No one complained at the time and that leads me to think this was cooked up after the fact.

MEDIATOR: I'm not asking you to agree on what happened before. An agreement about the past won't create a contract. I'm asking you to think about the future. We're trying to agree on how things will be dealt with in the future. If you got a grievance under this clause complaining about epithets or harassment by a conductor, wouldn't you want to investigate the matter?

EMPLOYER REPRESENTATIVE: Well, of course. If we received a grievance in these circumstances, we would certainly work to assure that any demonstrated problem was corrected. We don't want this kind of situation.

MEDIATOR: And if the problem could not be worked out, arbitration would be available. It would then be up to the arbitrator to decide, in light of the circumstances, what might be an appropriate remedy. Why don't you both consider this further in your next caucus?

UNION REPRESENTATIVE: We will; I think you've given us some new approaches to consider.

MEDIATOR: Where are we regarding the Union's concern over reassignment of principals for particular operas?

EMPLOYER REPRESENTATIVE: In light of the arbitration award that was rendered, we are prepared to acknowledge that the Opera must pay such a principal the wages they would have earned if the reassignment were not made. Specifically, we would propose adding the following language to the agreement:

> "Full compensation for service for which a principal is not assigned shall be paid. Full compensation shall include principal minimum scale, over scale payment, if any, plus any earnings that would have been earned had the principal not been moved (or not assigned to play)."

We feel this should be sufficient to solve the problem.

UNION REPRESENTATIVE: Well, it's not sufficient to solve the problem. The money is one thing, and we certainly welcome a commitment that no principal will suffer a loss of earnings as a result of a decision like this. But money is not everything. By imposing that remedy, the arbitration award really suggested that this should not have occurred in the first place. That's our view. As far as we are concerned, there should be no reassignments of principals. Having earned that job, they are entitled to perform it.

EMPLOYER REPRESENTATIVE: We simply can't commit to that kind of limitation. If the musical director decides that a different assignment is appropriate for a given opera, we don't want to be in a position where we have foreclosed that.

Flush out specific problems
<11>

MEDIATOR: (Speaking to the Union representative) You said that there is more at stake here than money. Precisely what is it in addition to money that is at stake?

UNION REPRESENTATIVE: Well, quite frankly, everyone in the musical community knows when something like this takes place. The principals affected may be right or wrong about what they conclude, but there is no question about how they perceive it. They believe that this injures their reputation. And we don't believe that a person's reputation should be unnecessarily injured in that way. It could affect their ability to get work in the future.

MEDIATOR: Let me make a suggestion here. As I read the expiring agreement, it states that players may file a grievance if they disagree with a change in seating made by the Employer. Both proposals continue that provision for the term of the new agreement. As I understand what the Union is saying, they are suggesting that a reassignment for a particular opera has many of the same effects as a permanent change in seating. At least, some of the musicians feel it affects their reputation in a similar way, even if it does not affect their earning ability. Now, maybe this problem could be solved by specifying that if the Opera reassigns a principal some specified number of times, this will be treated like a change in seating that is subject to grievance. That will require the Employer to justify what it has done, and it will give the affected employee an opportunity to respond to any of the criticisms that may have caused such a decision.

EMPLOYER REPRESENTATIVE: I think that's an idea worth exploring. As long as the Opera's right to do this on an occasional basis is protected, we would be willing to make further reassignments subject to the grievance procedure.

UNION REPRESENTATIVE: We don't like the idea of this taking place at all, but we would be willing to look at proposals along those lines. We'll have to see how much leeway is afforded to the Opera.

MEDIATOR: (Speaking to the Employer representative) Why don't you prepare a further proposal in this area during the next caucus session?

Further Developments: After further caucuses and joint sessions, the two issues picked for purposes of illustration were resolved. The Union withdrew its proposal regarding conductors, in reliance upon language of Article VI, guaranteeing its members "pleasant working conditions." The issue of reseating was resolved by adding language to the Opera's proposal stating that, should an individual be reassigned for more than two (2) operas in any performance year, further reassignment would be regarded as constructive reseating and subject to the grievance procedure.

Summary of Events
(Days Number 8 and 9)

The Mediator began discussion of noneconomic issues by asking the Union (who was the "moving party" as to nearly all of these issues) to list its highest priorities. As these were discussed, the Mediator made more use of joint meetings than he previously had. He concluded that less discussion took place about these issues during the negotiating sessions before mediation, and that joint exploration of the problems could be beneficial.

The Mediator used two primary methods to settle the most difficult noneconomic issues. First, he required the parties to identify the specific problems motivating each proposal. To do this, he had to divert them from the broad issues of "principle" addressed in some of the proposals and get them to talk about the specific facts that caused one side or the other to feel that a change was needed. Parties are not likely to concede matters of "principle," but they can be expected to solve specific problems.

Secondly, the Mediator assisted the parties in formulating solutions to the specific problems identified. He pointed out that language from the expiring agreement could be used to deal with the conductor issue without any new additions. And he also brought the old agreement to bear upon solution of the dispute over reassignment of principal musicians.

The Mediator's efforts produced settlement of all noneconomic issues by the end of Day Number 9.

These developments were discussed in the following conversation:

Private Conversation Following Settlement of These Issues

OBSERVER: I was quite fascinated by the progress of discussions regarding the conductor issue and the reseating issue. When these two issues first came up, the parties sounded so diametrically opposed that any chance of settlement was impossible. Did you have any hope that they could be resolved within two days?

MEDIATOR: I noticed one thing during the early discussion of these two issues. Both parties were speaking about large, sweeping issues of principle. As to the conductor issue, for example, the Union was speaking of its members' absolute right to be free from harassment. The Employer committee was speaking of the Opera's absolute right to manage. Of course, it's not to be expected that either side will succeed in persuading the other to adopt its principles. More wars have been fought and more lives have been lost regarding supposed issues of "principle" than anything else, and no one's opinion was really changed when it was all over.

OBSERVER: How do you handle that kind of situation?

MEDIATOR: The key in this kind of situation is to identify the specific problem that has led to a proposal. Many times, it is possible to address the specific problem and solve it, without requiring either side to change its principles. That is why in further sessions I encouraged the Union representative to identify what specific problems caused its committee to advance these proposals. I felt that identifying the Union's specific problems would improve our chances of bringing about a settlement on these points. And, as you witnessed, identifying the specific problems enabled us to assist in solving them.

Day Number 10

Further Developments: By the end of Day 9 all noneconomic issues had been resolved. The parties met on Day 10 to resume work on the economic package, which had been left up in the air in the early morning hours of Day 7. Because the Day 9 session ended quite late, the parties met at 11:00 A.M. on Day 10. The Mediator began on Day 10 by meeting with the Employer committee:

Meeting with Employer Committee 11:00 A.M.

MEDIATOR: My notes indicate that when we put the money issues on hold this is where things stood. Do these figures match yours? (The Mediator then confirmed the accuracy of the following notes.)

Mediator's Notes
(Day 7)

12:10 A.M. Employer Proposal:
  $800 / $850 / $900 per week
  Supplemental Guarantee
    $1,600 / $1,700 / $1,800 per year

1:10 A.M. Union Proposal:
  $800 / $885 / $975 per week
  Supplemental Guarantee
    $1,600 / $2,000 / $2,500 per year

EMPLOYER REPRESENTATIVE: Right. My notes show the same figures.

MEDIATOR: All right. They made the last move. Are you in a position to come up with a new proposal?

EMPLOYER REPRESENTATIVE: I think so. We didn't put out all our money for the second and third years of the agreement before because the deadline was still a week away. We figured we'd need something to work with later. Give us a few moments and we'll come up with something.

Don't allow the parties to lose momentum <9>

MEDIATOR: Before I leave, let me make a couple of suggestions. We've got a lot of momentum working for us now. All their noneconomic issues have been resolved and first-year money is settled. For the first time, they know a package can be put together without a strike, and excitement over that should inspire some movement from them. You could lose that momentum though. If they think you're dickering nickel by nickel, then they'll keep you here until Day 13 to make sure they've gotten every last penny.

EMPLOYER REPRESENTATIVE: What are you suggesting?

Uncover possible movement, and <18>

MEDIATOR: I'm suggesting this. If you haven't already done so, take some time right now to figure out exactly how much you can spend. Put it *all* out there. If I can tell them you've scraped the bottom of the barrel, then I think we can settle this thing.

EMPLOYER REPRESENTATIVE: Are you sure? We've always held on to a little something until the last minute.

Direct its use with careful timing <21>

MEDIATOR: You've told me that you want to wrap this up in time for a ratification vote before rehearsals are scheduled to start. If that's true, then you ought to make your best offer now. If you slow things down, you can count on them to do the same thing.

EMPLOYER REPRESENTATIVE: I see your point, but I think we'll need to talk among ourselves a bit.

Help construct salable proposals <19>

MEDIATOR: While you're thinking about it, let me give you something else to work on. Their first impression when they look at this proposal is going to be very important. I have an idea on format that may help sell anything you put together. Every proposal they have made has shown expected annual compensation at the bottom. It's very clear to me that they want to tell the membership everyone can count on making $30,000 per year by the end of the contract. When you prepare your proposal, put the expected annual earnings right up at the top. Total up everything: the time guarantees, the supplemental guarantee and the minimum vacation. Feature the total, and if you can get to $30,000 by the end of the contract, I think I'll have something I can sell.

EMPLOYER REPRESENTATIVE: It will take me a little while to do the math. I don't know if we can get to that figure or not.

MEDIATOR: Take whatever time you need because the move you make now will be very important. If there's any way you can reach that figure, do it. I'll give you some time to yourselves, but remember what I've said and feature the *total* annual earnings.

Further Developments: After two hours, the Employer representative informed the Mediator that the Employer committee had decided to take both of the Mediator's suggestions, and that the proposal would probably show expected annual earnings of $30,000 by the last year of the agreement. It looked as though the Employer Committee would need another two hours or so to finalize all the figures in its proposal. The Mediator explained to the Union representative that he was taking time to get the best possible proposal from the Employer group. At 5:00 P.M. the Employer representative passed the proposal below to the Mediator. The conversation that took place between the Mediator and the Employer representative about the proposal's terms is set forth immediately thereafter.

Employer Proposal
Day Number 10/5:00 P.M.

I. Total Compensation Guarantee

	Year 1	Year 2	Year 3
Tenured Player	25,000	27,000	30,000
Nontenured Player	23,000	25,000	27,000

All compensation generated by Employer (with the exception of Unemployment Insurance) shall be counted towards the Compensation Guarantee.

Included shall be earnings reported on W-2 forms generated by Employer and its Affiliates, media payments, and all payments whether made directly by the Employer or through another payor (e.g. a television program paid directly by a sponsor or station; an opera concern paid directly by a corporation, etc.)

All supplementary employment will be announced as soon as possible by Employer. If offered employment is refused by musician, the Compensation Guarantee will be reduced accordingly.

II. Rates

	Year 1	Year 2	Year 3
6 Services for 20 Weeks @	$800.00	$860.00	$920.00
12 Preliminary Days @	$133.33	$143.33	$153.33
85 Rehearsal Hours @	$ 27.00	$ 28.90	$ 30.90

III. Vacation
       a. Current System; with
       b. 1 week minimum for Nontenured Players;
       c. 2 week minimum for Tenured Players.

MEDIATOR: The $30,000 looks good. Can you explain the rest of this?

EMPLOYER REPRESENTATIVE: Yes, it's easiest if we start with the last item. As you know, their proposal for some time has been for a minimum of two weeks' vacation. Now we can do that for most of the musicians; we can certainly do it for the tenured group. But we can't go that far for the nontenured group.

Get the facts
<12>

MEDIATOR: How much service do they have?

EMPLOYER REPRESENTATIVE: Less than three years, in all cases. And no part-time Employer gives two weeks vacation to people with that little service. So we're suggesting one week for that group and two weeks for the rest.

MEDIATOR: Now how does that fit in with the total guarantee?

EMPLOYER REPRESENTATIVE: Just this way. We've

done what you suggested. The total amount they can count on making is featured at the top. That includes what they make working the time guarantees, the 20 weeks, 12 days, and 85 hours. It includes the minimum vacation, and since tenured and nontenured will be getting different minimum vacation, we've stated their total guarantees separately. And it includes the amount we were showing as a "supplemental guarantee" before *plus* a little bit more. But that little bit more is only possible if they accept this language counting *all* Opera-generated income toward the guarantee.

MEDIATOR: Does all this mean the tenured players can count on a guarantee of $30,000 by the end of the contract?

EMPLOYER REPRESENTATIVE: It does. As it turned out, treating the tenured and nontenured players in different categories was essential to reaching your $30,000 goal. We couldn't guarantee that for everybody. But we can for the tenured players because nearly all of them will continue to earn more vacation than the minimum guaranteed. What's out there is more than we intended to spend, but we've pushed up a bit in reliance upon your advice that getting to $30,000 will make a difference.

MEDIATOR: All right. Let me see what I can do with this.

Further Developments The Mediator then made copies of the Employer proposal and went in to meet with the Union. He did *not* pass around the written proposals immediately because he wanted to "set the stage" before doing so.

Meeting with Union Committee 5:30 P.M.

MEDIATOR: As you know, I've been working with them all day. I wanted to make sure the proposal I brought to you now cleaned their pockets. Let me tell you a few things about it before I pass it around. First, I've gotten them to simplify the guarantee issue. You'll see listed at the top the exact *total* amount that every musician can count on making. That's the main thing you've been asking for from the beginning. There's a category for tenured players and one for nontenured players. It includes everything: vacation, what you earn working the time guarantees, and what you can count on from extra work, *everything*. Now you'll see in the last year of the contract, tenured players are guaranteed $30,000. Getting them to that figure was no easy job. Simply put, we've scraped the bottom of the barrel. You're not going to see any more money than this, and it's an accomplishment to have that much in front of you. All right, let me pass this around and see if you have any questions. (A few moments then passed).

UNION REPRESENTATIVE: What's all this language after the guarantee?

> The mediator as a third negotiator
> <19>

MEDIATOR: The only way you're going to get any guarantee is if *all* Opera-generated income counts. That's what the language says. If you've got a problem with the specific terms, then raise it, but something has to go in there.

COMMITTEE MEMBER: We proposed a minimum of two weeks vacation for everybody.

> Make clear when there is no more to be gained by dickering
> <19>

MEDIATOR: That's right, and you're not going to get *that* without a strike. I'm not sure you'd even get it *with* a strike. The nontenured group has under three years of service, correct?

COMMITTEE MEMBER: Yes.

MEDIATOR: Well, their view is that one week is appropriate for that group.

UNION REPRESENTATIVE: Are you sure all the money is on the table?

MEDIATOR: I'm sure all the money *and then some* is on the table. I wasn't talking to myself between 11:00 and 5:00 o'clock you know. This is it. Look, I'm going to give you some time to yourselves. You've worked hard and you've accomplished a great deal. I'm going to suggest that you ought to think long and hard about prolonging this thing.

A Case Study 101

Further Developments: After the Union group had met for about an hour, the Union representative came in to speak with the Mediator alone, at which time the following conversation took place:

UNION REPRESENTATIVE: Look, I'd like to wrap this thing up, but I'm having a problem with the group. Some of them have been on prior committees, and they've always gotten a little more by holding out until the last minute. They just can't quite bring themselves to believe that this is really it.

MEDIATOR: Are these terms acceptable as far as you're concerned?

UNION REPRESENTATIVE: I think so, but everyone wants to do the best possible job for the members that we can.

> Explore options with spokespersons or others with insights about the group
>
> <18>

MEDIATOR: I have an idea. When we settled the pension issues, we were talking about a four-year contract with the regular contribution rate going from 8% to 8½% in the fourth year. Since then everyone's money proposals have shifted to a three-year contract. Now, if I can get the Employer group to go for the higher contribution rate of 8½% one year sooner, in the *third* year, do you think your committee would be willing to wrap up the whole deal?

UNION REPRESENTATIVE: I think so. They just want to feel like they've wrung one more thing out of them!

MEDIATOR: All right. I'm going to go in and talk with your group.

Meeting with Union Committee 7:30 P.M.

MEDIATOR: I understand you aren't quite sure you've really cleaned their pockets. Let me make sure you understand where we are. This year isn't like past negotiations. I wasn't there in the past! Before they put together this proposal, I worked very hard to make sure they understood certain things. They want a ratification vote before rehearsals are scheduled to begin. I convinced them that they wouldn't get that *unless* they put all their money in this proposal. I also pushed them up to a $30,0000 guarantee for the tenured group even though they didn't intend to go that far.

COMMITTEE MEMBER: We appreciate what you've done, we just want to make sure we've done the best job for our members.

MEDIATOR: All right. Let me make a suggestion. I haven't talked to them about it, but I'm going to make it anyway. When we settled the pension issue, we agreed to a regular contribution rate increasing to 8½% in the fourth year of the contract. Since then, we've gone back to talking about a three-year agreement. I'd be willing to talk to them about pushing that increase into the *third* year, a year earlier, if you can tell me that would settle the whole contract.

COMMITTEE MEMBER: Let's see. My notes show our prior deal on the contribution rate was 7½% / 7½% / 8% / 8½%. So you're going to talk them into going from 8% to 8½% in the third year of our deal?

MEDIATOR: I don't know for sure if I can do anything! What I'm asking you is, will you commit to a settlement if I can get to 8½% within a three-year contract? What do you say?

UNION REPRESENTATIVE: Are you personally sure this is the best we can do?

MEDIATOR: I am.

ALL COMMITTEE MEMBERS (in sequence): All right. We'll go for it.

UNION REPRESENTATIVE: If you give us the go-ahead, we'll schedule a ratification vote for tomorrow evening.

MEDIATOR: Let's see what I can do.

Meeting with Employer Committee 7:45 P.M.

EMPLOYER REPRESENTATIVE: What's been going on? Where are we?

MEDIATOR: This is where we are: if you can take care of one small thing, we'll have a settlement. When we settled the pension package we were talking about a four-year deal and the agreed contribution rate was 7½% / 7½% / 8% / 8½%. Since then, everyone has gone back to working on the basis of a three-year contract. So, we need to adjust the pension settlement. You had committed to reaching 8½% by the end of the contract. If you will agree to 7½% / 7½% / 8½%, they will accept your wage and vacation proposal. That will settle the entire contract.

EMPLOYER REPRESENTATIVE (picking up calculator): Small thing!?! That's no small thing! You told us to put all our money on the table and we *did*. We put some out there we hadn't meant to. There's no more in the bank. Let me figure out what kind of money you're talking about.

MEDIATOR: Look, you might just as well throw that calculator out the window, because it's not going to settle this contract. If you will agree to this suggestion, you have an opera season; if not, your first performance will be in jeopardy because there won't be any ratification before rehearsals are scheduled to start. It's that simple. That's what you ought to be thinking about. I imagine the harm a disrupted season would do to your fund-raising would cost more than increasing to 8½% in the third year.

EMPLOYER REPRESENTATIVE: Will this really do it? Will this really settle the whole contract?

MEDIATOR: It will.

EMPLOYER REPRESENTATIVE: All right. Where can we celebrate!

MEDIATOR: Not so fast! I'm going to call everyone together so we can confirm this in writing immediately.

Joint Session 8:00 P.M.

MEDIATOR: First, I'm going to pass around the last economic proposal so you can all initial it. I've written at the bottom, "Regular Pension Contribution Rate:"

Year 1	7½%
Year 2	7½%
Year 3	8½%

With that change, everything should be agreed upon.

Finalize the agreement in writing immediately
<24>

Now I know all of you are exhausted, but we have some very significant work left to do. I understand that the Union has planned a meeting for the purpose of submitting this settlement to its membership for a ratification vote tomorrow evening. I gather that the membership has been highly interested in these negotiations, and they will be going over the different parts of this settlement very carefully. I'm going to suggest that we all meet here tomorrow (Day 11), arrange for a typist, and jointly prepare a full and accurate clean copy of the settlement. We have memoranda reflecting the settlements on each individual issue, but those ought to be incorporated while everything is fresh in our minds. If we can produce a typed copy tomorrow that everyone agrees upon, that will put the Union committee in the best possible position to communicate the settlement to the membership as effectively as possible.

EMPLOYER REPRESENTATIVE: I am willing to do anything necessary to help this process along. As we mentioned at the beginning of the evening, we need to know by the morning of Day 13 where we stand, in order to determine whether rehearsals should begin.

Further Developments: The parties accepted this suggestion from the Mediator. During the evening of Day 11, a lengthy Union membership meeting was conducted at which the settlement was ratified. The parties met again on Day 12 for the purpose of finalizing incorporation of the settlement into a draft of the new collective bargaining agreement and proofreading that draft. By the evening of Day 12, a typed version of the new collective bargaining agreement had been executed on behalf of both parties. The agreement was finalized before the Employer's deadline, the morning of Day 13.

Summary of Events
(Day Number 10 and thereafter)

On the morning of Day 10, there was great cause for optimism. The pension package, first year economics, and all noneconomic issues were resolved. The Mediator did not allow loss of this positive momentum. Rather, he gave careful thought to how the Employer's next economic proposal should be packaged in order to assure its salability with the Union. He actively encouraged the Employer to put all its money on the table and to feature total guaranteed earnings of $30,000 by the end of the contract. He also actively persuaded the Union committee to accept this package.

In preparation for the prospect of a total settlement on Day 10, the Mediator had reviewed all memoranda of settlement on individual issues. This reminded him that the pension settlement was based on a four-year deal. He knew that this would have to be reconciled with later discussions before the day was over. When the Union committee expressed a need for some final concession before signing off, the Mediator was able to "kill two birds with one stone." He actively persuaded both sides to finalize an agreement on the basis that the final pension contribution increase would be advanced by one year.

Finally, the Mediator shepherded the process of assuring that a final, written agreement was prepared and signed by the Day 13 deadline.

These developments were discussed in the following conversation:

Private Conversation Late on Day 10

OBSERVER: Well, you really surprised me today. Things were going so well when we broke up last evening that I expected you to kick back and relax. Momentum was really working in your favor.

Learn about any prior history between the parties

<12>

MEDIATOR: That's right, and I wanted to make sure that momentum was used rather than lost. I had to keep in mind how these parties have behaved in the past. They have always dickered back and forth right up until the last minute. If I allowed that to happen again, there wouldn't be any written agreement before Day 13. I had to make sure the Employer put all its money on the table today, and I had to make sure it was packaged in a way that would be salable with the Union. We've talked for some time about the importance of that $30,000 plateau.

OBSERVER: Were you surprised that the Union bought a guarantee format just like the one they rejected on Day 3?

Be patient

<6>

Be patient

Be patient!

Make sure enforcement of the agreement is considered

<25>

MEDIATOR: Shall I say it one more time? Sometimes there simply is no substitute for the passage of time in mediation. This job requires patience more than anything else.

OBSERVER: You didn't seem so patient when you told the Employer Representative to throw the calculator out the window! And that's not the only time today you expressed a clear opinion. You were firm with both sides.

MEDIATOR: That's true, but there's something more important to remember. I didn't push anyone until I patiently educated myself about the issues and earned the respect of both sides. Without that, having clear opinion is not going to get a mediator anywhere. If I had not earned the Employer group's respect, I could not have counted on them to clean their pockets when I suggested it. And if I had not earned the Union group's respect, I could not have expected them to trust me that all the money was really on the table.

OBSERVER: I'm curious about one thing. Would you have handled these final stages any differently if you were dealing with some sort of dispute other than collective bargaining?

MEDIATOR: Like a lawsuit or a possible business deal?

OBSERVER: Yes.

MEDIATOR: Only in one respect. The importance of patience, building trust, and being persuasive at the right time are all the same. A mediator has to pay attention to one additional thing, however. Nearly all collective bargaining agreements have a built-in system for resolving problems if one side says the other is not complying with a settlement at a later point in time, say a year or two from now. Collective bargaining agreements usually call for arbitration to resolve the problem. The circumstances are different in other fields. When a child custody dispute is mediated, a court judgment is entered and the courts are available to enforce the arrangement if someone doesn't comply. Many times parties to a business transaction or civil dispute will not want to leave enforcement of their settlement up to courts. One side or both may feel that process is too time-consuming or unreliable. In that case, part of the mediator's job is helping the parties to develop their own process for resolving differences over interpretation or application of the agreement.

OBSERVER: That sounds like a rather minor part of the mediation.

MEDIATOR: It can be a very *major* part of the mediation. I mediated a civil dispute once in which there was such distrust that the plaintiffs would not even talk about a settlement until there was agreement on a fast, reliable method of enforcement.

OBSERVER: What did you come up with?

MEDIATOR: The parties wanted a fast system, but they also wanted to make sure that certain legal questions that might come up could be presented to a court. So we wrote a special procedure calling for a modified form of arbitration. It was agreed that the arbitrator's rulings on some issues could be reviewed in court.

OBSERVER: How did you sell the idea to the parties?

MEDIATOR: Well, the process was crafted to meet their particular needs, and that was its biggest selling point. Since I have considerable experience as an arbitrator, I was also able to talk convincingly to the parties about how to make arbitration useful.

OBSERVER: Your job certainly calls for some diverse skills.

MEDIATOR: I keep something on my desk you might be interested in. Bill Simkin is one of the country's most-noted labor mediators. This is what he wrote in his book about the traits a mediator should have:

In a semifacetious moment while preparing a speech in 1962, the author listed the following combination of qualities sought in a mediator:

1. the patience of Job
2. the sincerity and bulldog characteristics of the English
3. the wit of the Irish
4. the physical endurance of the marathon runner
5. the broken-field dodging abilities of a halfback
6. the guile of Machiavelli
7. the personality-probing skills of a good psychiatrist
8. the confidence-retaining skills of a good psychiatrist
9. the hide of a rhinoceros
10. the wisdom of Solomon*

OBSERVER: How does someone acquire all those traits?

MEDIATOR: Some of them you have to be born with; the others come with experience.

OBSERVER: But a lot of young people want to be mediators. Is there any way they can speed up the gray hair?

MEDIATOR: They should get in on the ground floor and represent people with problems that need solving. That's what I did. I learned a great deal about what happens to problems when people do not settle them voluntarily. That knowledge is now my best selling tool when promoting resolutions in mediation. I don't let people forget when the alternatives to settlement are less desirable.

OBSERVER: I have one last question for you. Did you make any mistakes in this mediation?

MEDIATOR: Simkin left out one thing: a mediator has to know how to keep secrets! If I made any mistakes, I'm not going to mention them.

---

*W. Simkin & N. Fidandis, MEDIATION AND THE DYNAMICS OF COLLECTIVE BARGAINING, 2d ed. (BNA Books, 1986), p. 43.

Chapter 2
Dissecting the Case Study: What Were the Keys to Success?

This chapter provides an ordered review of the skills and techniques displayed by the Mediator during the Case Study.

A. Improving Effectiveness—Setting the Stage for Success

Many people who study or analyze mediation are most interested in how the mediator handles those moments of high drama when conflict is apparent. This, however, is not an appropriate starting point. Whatever methods might be chosen in moments of high drama, the likelihood of success will be significantly affected by whether the mediator has or has not concentrated on some more subtle tasks at earlier stages of the mediation.

It is unquestionable that the behavior of human beings is affected by their surroundings. People who sit down to a table with paper plates and plastic forks act differently than people seated in front of china and crystal. In each instance, the host has consciously set the mood, and the behavior of most guests will be affected without their even thinking about it. In a mediation, the mediator is the host and the mediator establishes expectations.

To be as effective as possible, a mediator should consciously work to "set the stage for success"—to create a setting that fosters agreement. The range of issues that must be considered in order to fully set the stage for success is broad. Thoroughness is served by grouping them according to the device long used by journalists to assure a complete report—who, what, why, where, and when?

WHO?

1. Are All "Parties" Present at the Mediation Sessions?

Everything that transpires during a mediation is intended to alter the perspectives or positions of disputing parties so as to end the dispute. If persons whose views helped create the dispute do not directly participate, the mediation will be a waste of time. It cannot be expected to have an effect on absent people, and if the views of critical people remain unchanged, the dispute will persist.

Because of these simple facts, a mediator needs to think about whether anyone essential is missing at an early stage in order to "set the stage for success" rather than failure. Two aspects of this issue should be considered: the possibility of "missing parties" and the possibility of "missing persons."

Sometimes, a variety of parties are involved in a disputed question, and some, but not all, of them will seek mediation. If this occurs, it is absolutely critical for the mediator to help these initiating parties to identify all of the individuals or interest groups that could undermine a settlement by continuing to press claims through litigation or other means. Full implementation of any settlement will be most likely if such absent parties can be convinced to participate. If they cannot, this fact needs to be established early, so that special efforts can be made to identify and consider the interests of absentee groups and strive for a settlement that will not promote more argument rather than less.

The Mediator in the Case Study did not encounter a problem regarding "missing parties." The Opera and the Musicians Union were the only parties to the expiring collective bargaining agreement, and they were the only parties directly concerned with what the terms of a new agreement would be. The Mediator in the Case Study, however, did encounter a very close cousin to this problem, namely, the problem of "missing persons." Just as it is essential to have all parties represented in mediation, it is essential to assure that all persons who exert critical control over the positions adopted by parties participate directly in the mediation. If they do not, it cannot be expected that the positions of the parties over which they exert control will change.

When the Mediator first talked to each negotiating group separately, he sought to satisfy himself that those present would be in a position to control positions adopted by the parties, at least until the point when a proposed settlement would be returned to the Union's membership for a ratification vote and the Opera's Board for acceptance. He thought that this had been assured. In a short while, however, it appeared that the Employer's attorney was attempting to exert control over positions adopted by the Employer, even though he was not a direct participant in the mediation sessions. At this point, the Mediator quite properly encouraged the Employer either to involve its attorney directly in the mediation sessions or to limit his role to one of furnishing advice on questions of law, rather than furnishing advice about what positions should be taken. That suggestion was accepted, and the Employer limited its attorney's role to the supply of advice about questions of law.

The possibility of "missing parties" or "missing persons" must be considered by all mediators, no matter what the substantive nature of the dispute. Many authors have emphasized that when mediation of an environmental dispute is sought, the initiating parties generally do *not* represent all the interests that could undermine a settlement through litigation. These "missing parties" must be identified.

Lawrence Susskind, the Head of the Department of Urban Studies and Planning at Massachusetts Institute of Technology, describes a 1978 settlement concerning the then-proposed Grayrocks Dam project in eastern Wyoming. Environmentalists and Nebraska state officials challenged the project in court on the grounds that it would siphon too much water from the North Platte River. The environmentalists feared that this would alter habitat critical for the endangered whooping crane. When a solution to the controversy was negotiated, the participants were: the National Wildlife Federation, the National Audubon Society, the Powder River Basin Resource Council, the Laramie River Conservation Council (environmental groups); the State of Nebraska, the Wyoming Municipal Power Agency, the Rural Electrification Administration, the U.S. Army Corps of Engineers, the Land and Natural Resources Division of the U.S. Department of Justice (government agencies); and the Basin Electrical Power Cooperative (the developer).* It seems that the participation of everyone, apart from the whooping cranes themselves, was secured!

---

*Susskind & Weinstein, *Towards a Theory of Environmental Dispute Resolution*, 9 B.C. ENVTL. L. REV. 311, 322 (1980).

2. Working With a Manageable Number of Participants

The discussion above makes clear that mediation will not be successful if too few people are included. Likewise, success is hampered if *too many* people are included. Many times, the entourage that appears at a mediation session to act on behalf of a given party includes many people who do not exert actual control over the positions such party will adopt. Some may be there as resource people who have expertise concerning finances or other information to which decision-makers may wish to have access throughout the mediation sessions. Others may be there because they are regarded by the decision-makers as critical members of a constituency that must be satisfied. And, still others may be present, even though no one saw a particular advantage to their participation, simply because they injected themselves due to significant interest in the dispute or a personal agenda.

It is unquestionable that mediation is most effective when smaller numbers of people are involved. Before mediation, parties have typically been unwilling to compromise for fear that concession will not garner settlement, but rather demands for more concession. To overcome such obstacles, the mediator must promote candor in order to learn whether the candid expectations of the parties, which they have been unwilling to share with one another, contain a possible basis for settlement.

It is a simple fact of life that most people are more likely to be candid if they have a smaller audience, rather than a larger audience. They are more likely to discuss possible concessions if there are fewer potential critics within earshot. For these reasons, if any party to a mediation presents an unwieldy delegation, the mediator should take steps to reduce the critical participants to a manageable number. This may be done by suggesting that each party elect or designate a specified number of principal spokespeople. Sometimes it is helpful if this suggestion comes from the mediator, so that key representatives do not have to suffer political consequences for having reduced the role of anyone within their contingent.

Although most of the mediator's purposes are best served by reducing the number of direct participants, a counterpoint should be considered when determining the timing of any suggestion that the number of party representatives be reduced. That counterpoint is best summarized in a Chinese saying: "You cannot wrap fire in paper." Very frequently, persons involved in a dispute feel deeply that they have been wronged, and their paramount drive is for vindication.

Ultimately, they may see the wisdom of a settlement that includes accommodation, but work toward that goal cannot even begin until they feel assured that everyone is aware of the wrongs they have suffered. They do not want to see their "fire" disposed of lightly. And any attempt to ignore it, to "wrap it in paper," will fail.

This means that working groups should not be restricted in size until *after* a meeting attended by everyone has occurred, at which principal spokespeople explain the reasons for current positions of the parties to the mediator. This provides the principal spokespeople with an opportunity to demonstrate to everyone in their contingent that no one's "fire" is being "wrapped in paper."

In the Case Study, the Mediator began with a joint meeting of this type. Each principal spokesperson was given an uninterrupted opportunity to explain positions taken with reference to the outstanding issues. This resulted in some speech making and some expressions that could best be called "venting spleen" or "blowing off steam." The Mediator made a conscious decision to listen to some of this, rather than interrupting immediately, because experience had taught him that allowing the parties to vent some emotions can have important therapeutic benefits and may be essential before energies can be directed more constructively.

The Mediator did not need to suggest any reduction of the negotiating groups after this first session, since each began with a manageable number of representatives.

3. *Getting to Know the "Cast of Characters"*

Once it is determined who the critical players in the mediation will be, the mediator needs to begin acquainting himself with this cast. This is not something that is recommended merely for cordiality. It is essential in order to "set the stage for success."

In the Case Study, the Mediator made a point of meeting briefly with the committees representing each party immediately after the preliminary joint session. He did this for the purpose of beginning to acquaint himself with the "cast of characters." He pursued this part of his job as a two-way street, making some things about himself known and seeking information about the participants. The Mediator interjected references to his own past experiences, where appropriate, so that all participants would perceive his future advice as well grounded in considerable experience. He asked questions about the interests and priorities of individual participants so that he could weigh this information when making decisions about the timing or direction of future sessions.

The information that the Mediator learned while acquainting himself with the "cast of characters" was extremely useful and important. He learned that the Union committee consisted of two interest groups, one principally concerned about retiree benefits and the other principally concerned about wages. Perhaps most critically, he learned that both groups were resolved to support one another. This made clear that progress on both fronts would be needed in order to finalize a settlement. It also convinced the Mediator that he should be alert to possible conflict between the two groups and the prospect that one or the other group might need to be talked out of a position so extreme as to leave no funds available for satisfaction of other needs.

WHAT?

4. Joint Meetings Versus "Shuttle Diplomacy"

A mediator makes countless decisions about "what" is done in mediation sessions. One of those must be made as the stage is set for each major effort at progress. That is the choice between joint meetings, discussions with all participants present, and "shuttle diplomacy," an effort by the mediator to operate as an intermediary between groups working in separate caucus rooms.

Many of the factors bearing on this choice are discussed in the private conversation that took place at 11:00 A.M. on Day 3 in the Case Study. It is nearly always constructive to begin discussion of an issue in a joint meeting. This is most certainly true if the parties have not talked to one another at length about a particular question in the past, perhaps because their attention has been diverted by paramount issues. This situation existed in the Case Study with reference to the noneconomic issues. Since the parties were preoccupied with discussion of economic issues in their prior negotiations, they had exchanged very little information about the concerns that led to proposals on noneconomic topics. Joint meetings have utility as a starting point, however, even if past discussions between the parties have been extensive.

This is true for a number of reasons. One of the reasons is related above in this chapter under Section A(2) discussing "You cannot wrap fire in paper." A further reason applies in the case of nearly all disputes for which mediation might be attempted. Nearly all mediations are preceded by some effort of the parties to resolve their dispute without assistance through direct negotiation. This might suggest that each has heard a full explanation of the concerns advanced by their adversary, at least in connection with issues which have been extensively discussed. In light of human nature, however, this is rarely, if ever, true.

Each party may have stated its concerns in prior discussions, but this does not mean that their adversary heard the explanations given. In conversations between adversaries, it is quite frequent for hearing to become "impaired." People do not hear as well as they might because they are preoccupied with the merits of their own position and/or what they will say next. It is as though each side was speaking into a mirror, conscious of nothing other than their own image. A tendency to interrupt one another may also be a problem.

When a mediator is educated about the nature of the dispute through a preliminary joint session, each party must sit and listen to the other explain why it has adopted outstanding positions, and the mediator may *insist* that each party sits patiently during this period of time, rather than interrupting. The mere fact that each party has a dispassionate audience listening, namely, the mediator, affords each party a fuller opportunity to explain positions previously taken than is possible when the only audience present is one that is likely to respond antagonistically. The fact that all parties are present while this is happening assures that they will *all* hear one another's concerns a little bit more fully than they previously have. This is particularly true if the mediator begins to ask questions that will help identify the crux of the matter. Techniques for accomplishing this are discussed in Section B(11), below.

The private conversation of 11:00 A.M. on Day 3 refers to two additional purposes which may be served by joint meetings at later stages of a mediation. If serious questions arise about relevant facts, it may be helpful to bring the parties together so that the mediator may quickly hear what facts are agreed upon and what facts are a topic of dispute. Additionally, a joint meeting may be useful if all of the techniques summarized in this chapter are exhausted and an impasse nonetheless exists. If both parties have a significant incentive to settle and this incentive has been called to their attention, they will be hesitant to walk away from the table. Simply keeping them talking at this juncture may sometimes generate new movement or new ideas.

Although joint meetings are typically useful at the beginning, and for the specific purposes described above, many of a mediator's purposes are best served through "shuttle diplomacy." Candor is essential for effective mediation. The mediator must convince all parties to share more information and more willingness toward concessions than has previously been expressed. It is always easier to encourage such candor successfully when parties may explore thoughts tentatively in private. This is the principal utility of "shuttle diplomacy." As will be seen from the following discussion, much of what the mediator did in the Case Study would not have been possible without the use of "shuttle diplomacy."

WHY?

In most settings, there is no legal obligation to use mediation. This means that the parties have made a voluntary decision to try mediation. They must have done so because they anticipate that it can be of some help to them. This decision and expectation on their part creates some positive momentum which can be utilized constructively. There is no question, however, that the mediator must consciously do certain things in order to preserve this momentum and take full advantage of it.

5. Realistic Optimism—The Mediator Is Not a Magician

Most disputes cannot be settled without concessions. Parties are most likely to display possible movement if they believe that some concession on their part will inspire similar movement from the other side and make settlement a realistic possibility. Put simply, no one wants to waste a concession. No one wants to throw something away that will not contribute toward full resolution of the problem.

For these reasons, it is important that the mediator create an atmosphere of optimism and confidence that settlement is possible. The Mediator did much toward this end during the early stages of the Case Study. After he had heard a full explanation of the outstanding issues by the parties, he made a point of stating in everyone's presence that he had seen such problems resolved on many prior occasions.

The Mediator also took pains to preserve the optimism of the parties throughout the mediation. On a recurring basis, he called progress accomplished through mediation to the attention of the parties and emphasized what had been achieved. This was done to remind everyone that even if there was yet a gap to be bridged, progress was being made and further energy ought to be invested.

Throughout all of his efforts to preserve the confidence of the parties in the prospect of an ultimate settlement, however, the Mediator was also careful not to create any unrealistic expectations that could only lead to disappointment. He made certain that the parties were not expecting the Mediator to wave a magic wand over their circumtances and bring about a peaceful solution on his own initiative. He periodically reminded them that success would have to be the product of their own flexibility, thereby assuring that their optimism would be grounded in realistic expectations.

6. The Role of Patience—"You Cannot Eat a Hot Bun in One Bite"

This topic is closely related to the issue just discussed. Invariably, parties who begin participation in a mediation with optimism become, at some point, disappointed by what is perceived as a lack of movement from other participants. At such stages, it is part of the mediator's job to remind everyone that it takes nine months to make a baby. The mediator must not allow any party to become discouraged, but rather must refocus attention on areas where progress is being made and try to promote sufficient progress in those areas to finalize tentative agreement. If this can be accomplished, the resulting momentum will be of help in other areas where movement has not yet occurred.

The Mediator had ample opportunities to perform this function during the Case Study with reference to both parties. When the Employer assessed the Union's first full economic proposal on the morning of Day 4, it became indignant over the fact that the bottom line demanded just as much as the Union was demanding before mediation. Because he had totally analyzed this proposal before talking to the Employer about it, the Mediator was able to direct the attention of the Employer group to those aspects of the package which they might find most attractive and to suggest that those topics be made the focus for further discussions. In short, he reminded the Employer group that "You cannot eat a hot bun in one bite."

The Mediator performed a similar function during conversations with the Union group on Day 6, after the Employer reintroduced the notion of a supplemental guarantee. The Union was initially quite discouraged and unwilling to think about the concept, because the Employer was still insisting that any work which was turned down ought to be counted against the guarantee. Although the Mediator knew that this dispute remained outstanding, he encouraged the Union to focus upon the added money which was then being offered and determine if agreement might not be reached on the figure constituting an acceptable supplemental guarantee, pending finalization of the terms that would control payment of the guarantee. In both instances, the Mediator was preserving the optimism with which the parties began by reminding them that patience is essential to successful settlement of a problem.

7. *Obtaining the Trust of the Parties*

As already indicated, parties initiate mediation because they believe the mediator can accomplish something. In order to validate that expectation, the mediator must begin very early to confirm and build upon the trust of the parties. Many of the techniques which will be discussed in Section C of this Chapter require the parties to become candid with the mediator, sharing the rationales for their positions and concessions which may be possible under some circumstances. No mediator may presume that such trust will be automatic at the moment it is sought. Actions must be taken from the very beginning of the mediation to begin building this trust and "setting the stage for success."

Some of the things which a mediator may do to build trust have already been discussed. It is important for a mediator to find opportunities to discuss past experiences in order to make clear to the parties that advice given is grounded in experience. At the early stages of the mediation, it is also important for the mediator to adopt a somewhat less intrusive role than may become appropriate later. Thus, the parties are assured that the mediator has listened fully to their points of view before forming any independent point of view, and, as a result, they become more trusting of the mediator. No one likes to take guidance from someone who has less information about the problem than the combatants do.

While the foregoing points are important, they do not reach the crux of the matter where cultivation of trust is concerned. That is simple to state but more difficult to accomplish. Simply put, in order to build trust the mediator must make very effective use of the first candor displayed by the parties. If this may be done, it is certain that greater candor will follow. If this is not done, it is equally certain that the parties will begin to retrench.

Realizing this fact, the Mediator in the Case Study displayed extreme care when he sought to make use of the first information candidly shared with him by the Employer group. The Employer group shared that it might be willing to move to a formula of 60 percent times 38 years as the one-time payment for retirees *if* this concession became sufficient to wrap up a deal on the retirement issues. The Mediator went to considerable efforts, discussed more fully in Section C(19), to secure a commitment from the Union group that this concession *would* be sufficient before he pressed the Employer to commit to this formula as well. He was successful in securing such a commitment from the Union group, and this rewarded the Employer's trust. The Employer saw that its candid discussion with the Mediator produced settlement of an issue which the parties by themselves had found totally irreconcilable. Nothing fosters trust better than success.

Mediators must acknowledge this reality, and must proceed with particular care at the early stages of a mediation to assure that tentative expressions of trust are rewarded and built upon. This again makes patience a critical virtue in mediation.

WHERE?

8. *The Location of Meetings*

This may seem like a mundane topic, but it can be quite important to "setting the stage for success." The discussion above in Section A(4) concerning "shuttle diplomacy" makes clear that meetings must be scheduled where adequate rooms are available for all groups to engage in private caucuses. There is a further matter which ought to be considered when selecting the location for mediation sessions. Candor and movement will most likely occur if participants to a mediation session do not feel they are being scrutinized by potential critics. For this reason, it is best not to meet in a place where one or another group will likely be barraged with questions about progress of the mediation from members of a constituency. This can sometimes be a problem if representatives of a business entity meet on their own premises. The mediator needs to be alert to this possibility so that a neutral location where everyone will be insulated from such questions can be suggested.

WHEN?

9. The Order of Attack

Most disputes requiring mediation concern multiple issues. The mediator plays a critical role in determining when each of these various issues will become the focus of attention. Directing attention to a particular topic at one time may produce failure, while directing attention to it at another will produce success. It is part of the mediator's job to make judgments about when the probability of success concerning various items is greatest, and to guide the discussion accordingly.

On two different occasions in the Case Study, the Mediator suggested tackling the highest priorities first. He did this at the conclusion of the very first joint session. After hearing both parties explain their outstanding positions, he requested the Union to identify the demands on its part which were of greatest concern. During Days 7, 8, and 9, when attention was focused on noneconomic issues, the Mediator again asked the Union to identify those requests which it deemed to be most important.

This tactic might appear risky to some. Parties who fail in an effort to tackle the most important parts of their dispute have very little incentive to work through any remaining issues. The Mediator in the Case Study, however, did not pursue this course of action haphazardly without reference to those risks. He was aware of them, but he chose this course of action because of countervailing considerations. As already mentioned, parties begin their participation in mediation with a high degree of optimism. Because they expect progress to be made, they are slightly more forthcoming with potential movement on their own part. The Mediator was striving to capitalize upon this added flexibility and apply it where it was needed most, in connection with the high priority issues.

In a mediation where the behavior of the parties does not create grounds for such optimism, however, a different course of action is advisable. If the parties are so discouraged that they are reticent to display any movement, it is generally best to start with issues of lesser importance so that some confidence in the process can be built before the most challenging issues are approached. This is one of the many topics as to which the mediator must carefully analyze the behavior of the parties and follow the signals their behavior provides about what course of action is best.

It should be noted that the noneconomic issues in the Case Study became the focus of discussion in Days 7, 8, and 9 because of a further decision the Mediator made about the order of attack. He had taken time to educate himself about the past history of these parties during their negotiations, and he knew that they had never come to terms on economic issues until the last moment before expiration of a prior agreement. Because of this history, he knew that both sides would be hesitant to show their bottom line on economic issues while the deadline they faced was still some distance away. Rather than trying to immediately alter these established behavior patterns, he redirected their attention to noneconomic issues during Days 7, 8, and 9, since these needed to be resolved before the deadline as well. This decision on the part of the Mediator kept the parties working constructively throughout the mediation and prevented them from becoming too frustrated with their economic disputes, at a time when neither side could successfully be pushed the last distance necessary to bring about a settlement.

Just as it is important for the mediator to make strategic decisions about the order in which general topics are approached, it is equally important for the mediator to make strategic decisions about the order in which subordinate issues relative to a general topic are approached. In the Case Study, nearly every general topic included several subordinate issues. For example, the negotiations of the parties about the general topic of pension benefits raised questions concerning three types of subordinate issues: (1) the supplemental one-time benefit; (2) additional benefits and terms for all retirees; and (3) the regular contribution rate.

Each time either party communicated a change in its positions about these subordinate issues, the Mediator created careful notes so as to avoid any error in transmission. He would have created less work for himself if he had simply taken these careful notes and handed them over to the other participant in the mediation in order to communicate the changes which had taken place. While the Mediator could have minimized his work in this fashion, serving as such an "errand boy" would also have minimized his chances for success.

Disputing parties do not need a mediator solely to make accurate records of what they are saying and carry written messages between them. This really adds nothing to what disputing parties might be expected to accomplish *without* the assistance of any outsider and, indeed, these functions could probably be better accomplished by a stenographer. To enhance chances for resolution of the dispute, a mediator needs to be more than simply a scribe and messenger.

Each time that the Mediator in the Case Study created careful notes, he used the time to analyze what he was writing and plan his next move. When he approached the other party, he did not simply relate the contents of his notes. Rather, he chose the order of attack in a manner designed to enhance chances for a total settlement. The Mediator's use of the Employer's counterproposal at 4:30 P.M. on Day 3 is a good example.

That counterproposal contained positions about each of the three subordinate issues then being discussed in reference to pension benefits. Although the Mediator's notes set forth the Employer's position about the supplemental retirement benefit first, the Mediator did not begin by presenting this Employer position to the Union when he next met with them. He had formed an impression that this subordinate issue would be the most difficult one to resolve in the area of pension benefits. He also believed that the positions of the parties about additional benefits for retirees were sufficiently close to enable striking a deal on these points. Because of these two assessments, he began his discussions with the Union group by focusing their attention on the topic of additional benefits.

He had begun to implement a plan. His plan was to finalize agreement on everything except the supplemental retirement benefit, which he found to be the most difficult issue. This strategy was designed to build positive momentum that could be applied to the resolution of that difficult problem. He also refrained from communicating a concession the Employer had made about the regular contribution rate, because he foresaw that this concession might be needed at the last moment in order to inspire movement from the Union group. And this movement, in turn, would be essential in order to reach a resolution of the supplemental retirement benefit issue. In short, the Mediator had a plan and he chose the order in which subordinate issues were attacked so as to serve that plan and, thus, enhance chances for success.

Throughout the Case Study, the Mediator made similar strategic decisions about the order in which issues subordinate to a general topic ought to be approached. When he presented the Employer's final economic proposal to the Union group, he spent considerable time discussing critical characteristics of the proposal before showing anything to them in writing. The Mediator did this in order to emphasize the positive characteristics of the proposal so that the Union group would have these in mind as they looked at some details falling short of optimal goals.

B. Identifying the Conflicts

The fact that the "stage is set for success" does not mean that the mediator may immediately proceed to address areas of conflict. First, care must be taken to identify accurately what disputes really stand in the way of resolving the parties' problems. The time invested in this task is highly important, for it avoids wasting time in the discussion of irrelevant or unnecessary issues.

10. What Are the Issues as the Parties See Them?

For the reasons discussed above in Section A(4), it is usually advisable for the mediator to begin by listening to the parties' explanations of the positions they have adopted thus far and their reasons for doing so. Most parties will have more confidence in a mediator if that mediator has listened patiently to them before offering any guidance or advice. This step, however, must be regarded as the starting point, not the conclusion of the mediator's effort to gain an education about the issues in dispute.

In most instances, the mediator will hear this initial review of the issues in joint session. This review should always be supplemented by private conversations in which the mediator can encourage each party to share more candidly which issues are considered most important. After the Mediator in the Case Study conducted the first joint meeting, he initiated individual conferences with each negotiating group so that he could press for such candid discussion of each party's priorities. In both joint meetings and in individual conferences, the steps described in the next section become critical to accurate identification of the issues.

11. Peeling the Artichoke—Finding the Heart of the Matter

Some might suppose that parties who have been negotiating prior to seeking out mediation could be expected to understand their areas of dispute and describe them accurately. Curiously, this is rarely the case. One of the central reasons mediation can be helpful is that interested parties typically do a very poor job of identifying exactly what it is that they disagree about—what *needs* to be addressed in order to enable them to live peaceably together. Negotiating parties frequently need the help of an outsider, who has not become emotionally involved, to help identify the precise conflicts requiring resolution.

Negotiating parties tend to lose sight of the actual conflicts requiring resolution for two reasons, which may be called the "conversion problem" and the "blinders problem." Understanding these reasons can help the mediator overcome the obstacles to settlement which the parties have created.

The "conversion problem" is best illustrated by the position the Union in the Case Study took prior to mediation about selection of conductors. Specific facts happened which caused the Union to conclude that a problem existed requiring correction. Those events consisted of insults and profanity on the part of one conductor. The Union negotiating group applied its values and principles to this problem in order to come up with a proposed solution. It determined that management was not doing an adequate job of screening unacceptable conductors and that the orchestra itself ought to be given the prerogative to disqualify any offending conductor from future employment. As a matter of principle, the Union negotiating group deemed the orchestra better qualified to make an employment decision in this circumstance than management.

When the Union negotiating group applied its values and principles to this question, it *converted* an issue about a specific factual problem into an issue of principle. The proposal it put on the table demanded the right to control employment of conductors. The Employer committee saw this proposal as inimical to its strongly held values and principles, including the proposition that employment of conductors is a management prerogative of the Opera.

At this stage, the "conversion problem" had set the stage for failed negotiations, and the Employer group fell prey to the "blinders problem," thereby guaranteeing failure. The Employer group heard the proposal for orchestra control over employment of conductors. It considered this to be an outlandish demand premised on unacceptable principles. The ire of the Employer group was evoked, and it rejected the proposal emphatically. The anger of the Employer group, however, caused more than simply this rejection. That anger also created "blinders," which prevented the members of the Employer group from seeing any aspects of this issue apart from the unacceptable proposal which was the source of their indignation. They were resolved to reject the demand, and they had neither the interest nor the motivation to broaden their range of sight and search to discover what might have motivated such a position on the Union's part.

The approach the Mediator used in the Case Study concerning this issue illustrates what may be done when a mediator encounters the "conversion problem" or the "blinders problem." The Mediator pressed the Union group to do more than simply state its proposal and make laudatory speeches about that proposal. He pressed the Union representative to identify what factual events had been seen by the Union members as problematic, that is, what specific problem caused the Union to conclude that some proposal ought to be made. This caused the Union representative to explain for the first time across the bargaining table that a particular conductor had used language thought by the members of the orchestra to have been profane, insulting, and harassing. For the first time the parties focused attention upon factual events, rather than a dispute over principles.

Once this had been accomplished, the Mediator then helped the Employer group to remove its blinders. He directed their attention to these asserted factual events and encouraged the Employer group to think about whether some response might be possible, presuming the particular response suggested by the Union to be unacceptable. Ultimately, this guidance from the Mediator enabled the parties to resolve this issue. Before any progress could be made, however, the Union group had to be dissuaded from converting a factual problem into an issue of principle, and the Employer group had to be persuaded to remove its blinders and see that the actual problem was one that could be resolved.

In sum, the Mediator helped the parties "peel the leaves from the artichoke" in order to get to the heart of the matter. This is a task which must be performed on a recurring basis in mediation. Any time any party puts forth a seemingly unacceptable position, questions must be asked to find out what specific interests or problems have motivated that proposal. And the attention of other parties must be focused upon the problem identified, rather than the initial, unacceptable solution which has been put forth for that problem.

12. *Pressing for Known Facts and Discovering Unknown Facts*

As the section immediately above makes clear, very frequently peeling away the leaves of the artichoke and identifying the heart of the matter will lead to discussion of a specific past event. At this stage, it is important to have a full discussion of the facts in order to define the extent of conflict between the parties. The mediator should assure that this happens by asking each party to set forth the relevant information of which they are aware.

The Mediator in the Case Study did this on an ongoing basis. It first proved helpful in the initial joint meeting. In that meeting, the Union identified the topic of pensions as its highest priority. In order to reveal the underlying conflict, the Mediator pressed the Union's spokesperson for an explanation of the specific problem or problems which caused the Union negotiating group to give this topic highest priority. In response to the Mediator's urging, the Union's spokesperson explained that musicians with lengthy service retiring in the near future would receive very little because the pension plan had not been in effect for very long. At this stage, the Employer representative succumbed to the "blinders problem." The Employer spokesperson adamantly rejected the proposal which the Union had on the table for dealing with this issue, and refused to see or speak about the factual description of the Union's perceived problem, which was expressed at the urging of the Mediator.

The Mediator then directed the attention of the Employer group to the factual information which had been elicited from the Union spokesperson. He specifically asked the Employer representative to react to that factual description by explaining whether it comported with the facts as known by the Employer group and whether the Employer group could agree that some response to this scenario would be appropriate. In this instance, once the Employer group was required to focus upon the factual information which was underlying the Union's position, everyone discovered that there was vastly more agreement between the parties than had previously been perceived. The Employer group had no disagreement with the Union group about the operation of the pension plan, its effects, or other relevant facts. In this instance, the Employer was willing to agree as well that something additional needed to be agreed upon for musicians with long service who would receive only small benefits under the existing pension plan. In short, tremendous progress was made solely by guiding the parties to share their perceptions of the facts which had caused the Union to put forth a proposal for change.

Obviously, situations may arise in which disputing parties have different perceptions of relevant facts. In such a case, it is appropriate for the mediator to facilitate some sharing of information across the table in order to determine whether a basis exists to change the impression of one or the other party. For example, in the situation just described, if the Employer had disagreed about the operation of the plan, it would have been appropriate for the Mediator to request the Union to put forth more detail about the basis for its factual conclusion. The Mediator may have suggested to the Union that it use one or two musicians as examples and generate more detailed computations reflecting the economic circumstances of those persons. Review of such information at the bargaining table can have a number of positive consequences. It may actually change the perception a party has about the facts. On other occasions, it may be what is needed in order to press a party into abandoning what was a factually indefensible position from the beginning, adopted solely in the hope of stalling or sending up a smoke screen. Because such "information sharing" can be helpful, it should be initiated by the mediator whether the issue on the table concerns past factual events or the factual feasibility of proposals for future action.

Factual information known by the parties which they may be encouraged to share across the table is not the only sort of factual information which may be useful in narrowing areas of conflict. Indeed, frequently the facts which may be most helpful in narrowing areas of conflict are facts which the parties themselves have failed to notice. This happens because negotiating parties may become preoccupied with defending the positions they have previously taken rather than exploring for relevant facts that may point to alternatives. As an added party to the negotiations, the mediator may assist in the discovery of helpful facts. In order to accomplish this, the mediator should prepare by walking all of the ground that should have been walked by each party or their spokesperson. This includes thinking through the ramifications of all positions previously taken and learning as much as possibly can be learned about the parties' past dealings. This sounds tedious, but there is no short-cut means of unearthing potentially helpful facts which may have previously escaped everyone's attention.

In the Case Study, hard work of this nature paid tremendous dividends for the Mediator. Before the mediation sessions progressed, he took the time to read the expiring agreement between the parties carefully. Because he did this, all of its terms were fresh in his mind. After he peeled the leaves of the artichoke to discover the factual basis for the Union's proposal about selection of conductors, he was able to call everyone's attention to a provision within that agreement about which they had forgotten. He reminded them that the Union and its members already had the right to grieve or complain against any "unpleasant working conditions," which meant, in essence, that the Union already had a means to deal with this kind of problem. Direction of attention to this fact made it possible for the parties to conclude that in reality no conflict existed which required immediate resolution. The efforts of the Mediator to educate himself about potentially relevant facts that others may have missed enabled the parties to reach this conclusion.

While discussion of factual matters may have all of the positive benefits described above, there is a counterpoint which should be noted at this juncture. On occasion in negotiations, parties will become bogged down in an irreconcilable difference of opinion over some past event. A mediator should strive to keep factual discussions focused and constructive. If both facts known by the parties and facts newly brought to light by the mediator have been brought to bear without success, then attention should quickly be shifted to an alternative means of accomplishing settlement, before the parties become too antagonistic. The mediator must keep in mind at all times that there are alternative routes to settlement. Frequently, there is no necessity for the parties to come to complete agreement about what has happened in the past. They may resolve current differences as long as they are able to agree about what will happen in the future. When an issue fits into this category, the mediator should remember that it may be more constructive to focus the attention of the parties on their future conduct, than on what has happened in the past.

The Mediator in the Case Study refocused the attention of the parties to the future at a different critical stage of the discussion about the Union's proposal over employment of conductors. The Employer representative had made clear that the Employer group was not prepared to accept the representation of the Union group about what may or may not have been done by prior conductors. The Mediator then quickly concluded that such acknowledgment was not essential to a settlement. The Union was not requesting anything designed to compensate its members for wrongful treatment that had happened in the past. It was only asking that steps be taken to avoid similar conduct in the future. Because settlement of this issue appeared possible by focusing attention on the future conduct of the parties, rather than allowing them to dwell on the past, the Mediator pressed the Employer representative to think about whether the Employer could feasibly commit to a course of action in the future that would satisfy the Union's needs. In this situation, the tactic used by the

Mediator was far more profitable than lengthy discussion of past facts would have been.

C. Resolving the Conflicts

Although resolution of conflict is the part of mediation which people tend to find most interesting, a mediator who begins at that step without working on the prior steps discussed in parts A and B of this Chapter will not have a high probability of success. Once the stage has been set for success, however, and the mediator has done everything possible to help the parties better identify the disputes really standing in the way of resolving their problems, it is time, as they say in Montana, to "get down to the nut-cutting."

13. *Bringing the Facts to Bear*

As Section B(12) above makes clear, sometimes requiring the parties to focus on the facts relevant to a demand can cause a presumed conflict to disappear. This was true concerning the Union's demand to disqualify certain conductors from future employment. At the Mediator's urging, the Union thought about the nature of the events generating this demand and the nature of its current rights under the collective bargaining agreement. Once it had brought these considerations to bear, it found no need to continue pressing a demand for new rights.

These steps, however, are not always sufficient to resolve a conflict. Sometimes, even though attention is focused on relevant facts which should cause one or another party to change their position, that party may be unable or unwilling to see the significance of the fact on the table. In such a case, the mediator should not hesitate to speak persuasively to such party about the impact of the facts on outstanding positions.

The Mediator in the Case Study was required to use powers of persuasion in connection with the Union's demand for contract language guaranteeing that principal musicians would not be reassigned for particular operas. During the term of the last agreement a dispute over such a reassignment had gone to arbitration and an award had been rendered giving the reassigned principal musician all of the monetary benefits that would have been earned if the reassignment had not taken place. This award was based on a finding about the reassigned musician's contractual rights. Although attention was focused on this relevant fact by the Mediator, the Employer refused to acknowledge that such an award ought to have any impact on its bargaining position. It suggested that since the Union had prevailed in arbitration, the Union simply ought to stand ready to file a grievance and proceed to arbitration any time such a principal musician might be reassigned in the future.

This response, however, was a highly inefficient one. Parties negotiating a collective bargaining agreement ought to strive to conserve their resources and reach agreements that will minimize any need to use the arbitration process. The Mediator spoke persuasively to the Employer committee and pressed it to consider realistically the relevance of this past arbitration award to the Employer's position. He encouraged the Employer to recognize that an arbitration award will generally serve as precedent in a future dispute if the parties and issues are identical and if no change has been made in the terms of their contract. The reality of this fact and the advisability to both parties of avoiding arbitration costs during the term of an agreement both suggested that a change in the Employer's position was warranted. The Mediator's persuasive remarks to the Employer committee about these facts ultimately evoked a change in the Employer's position, and it agreed to provide reassigned principal musicians with their usual monetary benefits in the future. This change in position was a very significant step toward full resolution of the dispute between the parties over reassignment of principal musicians.

An important feature should be noted concerning the method used by the Mediator to persuade the Employer committee about the significance of these relevant facts on this occasion. Most of the discussion concerning the noneconomic issues took place in joint sessions because the parties had not spoken at any length about these issues during their negotiations prior to mediation. When the Mediator saw a need to speak to the Employer committee about the significance of the arbitration award, however, he made a very intentional decision to do this during a private caucus with the Employer committee. He did this because he anticipated that he would need to lean upon them rather heavily and speak forcefully. He knew that if he were to do this in the presence of the Union committee, the Union committee would become even more convinced that its position was a proper one which ought to be clung to until the bitter end. If this were to happen, it could create problems because the Mediator had no cause to be certain, as yet, that he would succeed in his efforts to persuade the Employer committee about the significance of the arbitration award. He did not want to boost unnecessarily the confidence of the Union committee before he knew that he could deliver. For these reasons, he was careful to initiate his efforts at persuading the Employer to find significance in the arbitration award during a private caucus session. He was additionally mindful of the fact that parties are always more likely to disclose some open-mindedness in a private caucus where there need be no fear that concessions tentatively expressed will be pounced upon by one's adversary.

14. Converting "Agreements in Theory" to Agreements in Fact and Firming Up Tentative Agreements

As discussed immediately above and in Section A(7), in order to evoke candor, a mediator must work to give parties the surety that they may discuss tentative concessions without fear that their adversary will immediately pounce upon them, giving nothing in return.

The mediator, however, should engage in some forms of "pouncing" in order to help the parties resolve their total conflict. The Mediator in the Case Study "pounced" in two different types of situations.

The first type of circumstance involved expressions of "agreement in theory." On a recurring basis during the mediation, the Mediator's efforts succeeded in causing one party to express general agreement about the facts or problems being described. The first example occurred in the very first joint session. The Union defended its pension proposal by explaining that musicians with long service who retired in the near future would receive a very small benefit because of the recent implementation of the pension plan. At first, the Employer expressed nothing but opposition to the Union's proposal. When the Mediator directed the Employer's attention to the specific problem described by the Union, however, and asked the Employer to express whether it agreed or disagreed concerning the existence of that problem, some progress occurred. The Employer not only recognized, as urged by the Union, that musicians with long service would be retiring with a comparatively small pension benefit, it also expressed the desire to do something for this group of people. This recognition by the Employer was certainly helpful, but of and by itself it did not bring about a resolution of any specific conflict on the table. The Mediator, however, used it as a building block to create a settlement of this issue.

He highlighted for both parties the extent to which they had expressed agreement in theory, and he encouraged the Employer to determine exactly how much money it could spend for this group of musicians and to create a specific proposal setting forth the manner in which the Employer might spend it. In short, he encouraged the Employer to convert this agreement in theory to a concrete proposal that could be the basis for further discussions. Throughout the Case Study, the Mediator kept his ears open for similar expressions of agreement in theory, and he consistently encouraged the parties to draft specific proposals embodying such agreements so that discussions could progress toward a full resolution of the issue involved.

On those occasions when the parties reached full agreement on all details necessary to resolve a given issue, the Mediator engaged in a similar form of "pouncing." He might have postponed all paper work until the conclusion of the mediation. He rejected this alternative, however, because he wanted to make certain that no confusion arose about the nature of tentative agreements that might stand in the way of a final settlement. For this reason, as soon as an issue was resolved, he made certain that the resolution was memorialized in a written document and initialed by all parties. The Mediator made clear the importance of this step at the conclusion of the first session on Day 3.

The parties had put in a very long and full day working toward resolution of all retirement issues. They were, in all likelihood, quite exhausted. Nonetheless, the Mediator made certain that the nature of the settlement reached on those issues was immediately reduced to writing. He further made sure that everyone had copies of a single document reflecting that settlement. He wished to make certain that a full settlement between the parties would not become threatened because one of the parties recalled the results of their discussions on retirement issues differently.

The remainder of the specific techniques discussed in Part C of this Chapter are available as possible tools that may be used to bring the parties to the point of agreement when neither "agreement in theory" nor "tentative agreement" has been expressed.

15. *Creativity—How Does the Mediator Promote New Ideas?*

Section B(11) (Peeling the Artichoke) illustrates that sometimes finding the heart of the problem also solves the problem. When everyone learned that insults and profanity by one conductor had motivated the Union's proposal on disqualification of conductors and the Union committee learned that language being retained in the new agreement would enable it to seek a remedy against such conduct, there was no longer any need for the Union to press its proposal. Properly identifying the underlying events and the facts relevant to them brought about a complete resolution of the issue. Properly identifying the problem underlying a dispute, however, does not always present an immediate resolution. In this instance, if the agreement had not contained language allowing the Union to seek a remedy if denied "pleasant working conditions," then full discussion of the facts would not have produced a solution to the conflict.

This is a frequent scenario in negotiation and mediation. Identifying the problem which has caused one party to make a proposal, and agreeing that it is a problem which ought to be addressed in some way, does not generally lead to an immediate solution. Most frequently, the solutions which have been offered thus far are deemed unacceptable by one party or another. Simply put, the ideas on the table—the old ideas—are not working. One party or the other believes that they create unacceptable consequences. Therefore, the parties must create new solutions for identified problems that do not result in consequences unacceptable for any of the parties.

Quite often, the parties directly interested in negotiation of a problem do not bring their creative powers to bear as efficiently as they might. There is a great tendency for parties who are suffering from the "blinders problem" to rest on statements opposing solutions which have been suggested rather than straining to formulate alternatives that might be palatable. There is a great need, therefore, for mediators to find creative solutions which will satisfy all parties.

This is hardly a difficult proposition to state or accept. New ideas are always of some potential help if old ideas have failed. It is difficult to learn, however, how a mediator may become more creative if creative ideas are not flowing naturally.

Examining the creative ideas suggested by the Mediator in the Case Study provides some excellent guidance as to how a mediator's creativity may be enhanced. The parties made great progress in discussion of retiree benefits, but they reached a logjam in their efforts to agree on a formula for computing the one-time supplemental payment to be made to retirees. During the late afternoon of Day 3, the Employer was insisting that the formula not exceed 50 percent of the musician's weekly salary multiplied by total years of service, not to exceed 40 years. The Union had originally proposed that this formula include a percentage figure of 100, but they had adjusted their demand downward to 75 percent. The Union was, however, refusing

134 THE ANATOMY OF MEDIATION

to budge any lower than 75 percent. After great progress, the parties appeared to be at an impasse. The gap between the Employer's position of 50 percent and the Union's position of 75 percent could not be bridged. The Employer had offered to adjust its cap on total years of service upwards to 45, but this possible concession had not interested the Union. It did not seem to care where the cap on total years of service was set.

Ultimately, the Mediator directed the Employer's thinking toward a creative approach which could be used to bridge the gap. The thought process displayed by his suggestion is extremely important. At this point, the parties had convinced themselves that no change in the cap on total years of service would help break the logjam. They were assuming that since the percentage figure was the only figure in dispute, movement would have to be made there, and only there, in order to break the logjam. The Mediator was able to suggest a new idea because he *questioned* in his own mind the unspoken assumptions that everyone else was making. He questioned the assumption that no change in the cap on total years of service would help. This led him to ask the Employer,

"Is there any way that you can increase the percentage by some amount and stay within your budget, perhaps by bringing the maximum years of service down a bit?" (See Meeting with Employer Committee, 5:30 P.M., Day 3.)

The Employer had stated firmly it could not spend any more money. Through this question, the Mediator was suggesting that the Employer might be able to put forth a new, more acceptable proposal without spending any more money by bringing the cap on years of service down slightly in order to permit pushing the percentage figure up slightly. This new idea was ultimately quite critical to solution of the entire retirement benefits package.

The thinking that produced this new idea is representative of the creative process. Creativity occurs when existing assumptions are challenged and, when appropriate, rejected. If the creative juices of participants to a mediation are not flowing well, the mediator may assist by privately making a conscious effort to inventory everything that is being assumed with reference to a given issue. If each item on that laundry list of assumptions is individually considered and challenged, very frequently one may find the seeds of a positive new idea.

The Mediator displayed how challenging assumptions can produce successful new ideas on a second occasion during discussion of retiree benefits. During the same meeting with the Employer committee, beginning at 5:30 P.M. on Day 3, the Employer expressed opposition to the Union's proposal for increasing the regular pension contribution rate to 8½% by the conclusion of a three-year agreement. Again, both parties were making an assumption. They were assuming that the new agreement would be for a term of three years. This left them with no alternative but to dicker back and forth regarding the percentage level of contributions. The Mediator questioned this assumption. He asked whether it might be possible for the Employer to increase the contribution rate to 8½% if the agreement was for a term of four years and the increase did not come until the fourth year. This new idea was also important to resolution of the pension issues, although the parties ultimately adjusted back to a three-year agreement.

The important fact to note, however, is that the Mediator was able to give the parties a useful new idea by questioning the unspoken assumptions that everyone was making. Experience and insight are very helpful in exposing unspoken assumptions that limit negotiating parties to a range of unacceptable options. In situations where experience and insight prove insufficient, however, there is no substitute for hard work. The mediator must take advantage of breaks between discussions to sit down and consciously identify the assumptions that are common to everyone's positions, question those assumptions, and search for new ideas.

16. Horsetrading—Finding Agreeable Exchanges

The technique just discussed is helpful if peeling the artichoke exposes a problem and everyone is willing to do something about it if a solution without unacceptable consequences can be found. Sometimes, however, one party to a mediation will *not* agree that the situation lying at the heart of the a dispute *is* something that the parties ought to address through a new commitment. The responding party may not be willing to agree that there is any problem requiring action. When this is the situation, and the relevant facts do not afford a basis for the mediator to seek a change in position, the mediator needs a different strategy.

It is helpful for the mediator to begin by making an assessment as to whether the topic is a major one or a lesser one. If it is a major one, then the remaining techniques discussed in this Chapter will need to be employed. If it is a minor one, however, the benefits of "horsetrading" should not be ignored.

Parties are rarely willing to drop a demand simply because opposition is stated, no matter how minor the issue might be. Parties typically want to feel that they have garnered something for the effort invested in a proposal. A mediator may accommodate this basic need by putting together package deals in which each party is asked to take some unacceptable demands of equivalent importance off the table. Frequently, a party who has been unwilling to withdraw a lesser demand, even though it is clear it has no chance of acceptance, will do so if the other party retracts a similar demand. Both sides will adjust their position if they see that progress is being made and that their movement is contributing toward a mutually acceptable settlement.

The Mediator in the Case Study isolated a package of such fair exchanges during discussion of retiree benefits. He convinced the Employer committee to maintain its prior benefit proposals (continuing medical coverage for retiree and spouse, instrument insurance, and dress rehearsal tickets) if the Union committee would withdraw its demand for dental coverage. He then strongly encouraged the Union committee to see this trade-off as an appropriate one which should be accepted. The success he achieved in creating this package, calling for equal movement from each side, resolved a significant number of outstanding retirement issues.

17. What Are Each Party's Pressure Points?

If conflict remains on major issues after all of the steps previously described have been employed, the mediator must become a more active "third negotiator," advocating on behalf of a possible basis for settlement. This is the primary topic of Section C(19), below. In order to accomplish this, however, the mediator must give thought to two preliminary issues: (1) What are each party's pressure points? and (2) What is in each party's "secret heart"? These are the topics of Sections C(17) and (18) because they are questions which must be considered before the mediator may pursue efforts as a "third negotiator."

First, the mediator needs to find pressure points which may be brought to bear in order to convince parties to change their positions. Frequently, the alternatives each party will face, if they are unable to reach a negotiated solution, provide the greatest source of pressure points. If those alternatives are harsh, in fact more harsh than what is being proposed at the bargaining table, then the mediator has an excellent basis to persuade reticent parties that some change in position is sensible. In such a circumstance, the mediator is basically urging negotiating parties to recognize that swallowing a small pill makes more sense than abandoning negotiations where the alternative is a larger pill.

In collective bargaining negotiations, the prospect of a strike is generally the big pill that all parties need to have in mind. Where Employees have the right to strike, as they do in the private sector, a work stoppage is the paramount alternative to a negotiated settlement. While all parties should be aware of this fact, they will sometimes forget the possibility of a strike when tenaciously asserting their various positions. The mediator may need to remind them of the costs associated with a strike and encourage them to take this into account when assessing whether various proposals should be accepted. This is true for both sides. It usually takes employers a long time to recoup business and profits lost by a strike. Likewise, it takes employees a long time to recover earnings lost during a strike.

In other cases, where the alternative to a negotiated settlement is court litigation, the mediator will need to remind each party of the costs associated with that option. Delay, attorney's fees, and the uncertainty of the result to be received in court are all "pressure points" which the mediator may bring to bear when helping the parties consider whether the solution available to them at the bargaining table is better than the alternative they face.

Mediators may find pressure points from sources other than the alternative facing the parties should negotiations fail. If the parties have common concerns, which have taken a back seat because of the present dispute, reminding them of those common concerns can frequently create pressure points useful to the mediator. Commercial parties frequently have an interest in maintaining a continuing relationship because they are useful to one another in their business enterprises. Sometimes, however, negotiating parties will forget this long-term goal and become intransigent over a current dispute in a way which harms these long-term interests. In this circumstance, the long-term goals of the parties are pressure points which the mediator ought to bring to bear when counseling them about the advisability of their current positions. If a dispute is allowed to persist or it produces litigation, the resulting animosity may impair the success of continuing business relations. The desire to avoid this can evoke the compromises necessary to enable a cordial conclusion to the dispute in mediation.

A very similar circumstance arises in mediation of child custody matters. Generally, each parent will state that the parent desires the happiness of the child. Frequently, however, they will have made their child or children pawns in a struggle to express hostility toward each other. In such a circumstance, the mediator must help the parents see the extent to which their conduct and positions are causing stress and insecurity to the child whose interests everyone says they have at heart. The mediator needs to make this common concern a pressure point that can bring about a change in attitude and position.

18. Discovering Each Party's "Secret Heart"

It is no secret, of course, that the positions stated by negotiating parties at the bargaining table frequently include "false bottoms." Parties frequently do not disclose their true bottom line because they hope to reach the most lucrative deal possible. Because of bartering custom, they may also feel that some flexibility must be preserved. Where these philosophies leave the parties some distance apart, however, a participating mediator must take steps to discover each party's "secret heart" in order to determine whether a settlement is possible.

The discussion included in Section A(7) (Obtaining the Trust of the Parties) is most crucial to setting the stage for accomplishment of this objective. The parties will not make candid disclosures to a mediator unless they trust that mediator, and the mediator must cultivate such trust from the very beginning of the mediation. As explained in that Section, it is most critical for the mediator to make careful use of the earliest candid disclosures made. It is almost essential that some success be accomplished as the result of such first candid disclosures. Nothing cultivates more candor than success, and nothing stymies candid disclosures more than their misuse.

Once trust has been cultivated, the mediator should act upon it by asking the parties whether there is some possible ground for movement which has not yet been disclosed. This may be done in individual caucus session or by taking a party's principal spokesperson aside. The mediator should inquire frankly and make no bones about it. This information is needed to discover whether there is a possible ground for settlement.

It can be helpful for the mediator to suggest a possible concession in such candid discussions to see whether it receives a good or bad reception. The Mediator in the Case Study did this successfully at the very beginning of Day 6. The Employer committee furnished him with a proposal in which the base rate for the first year of the agreement remained unchanged at $795. The Mediator felt that the Union committee had made very substantial concessions and that a proposal of $800 from the Employer on this item would be very likely to result in a settlement of the initial-year base rate. Before passing the proposal to the Union, therefore, he pressed the Employer representative to disclose whether it had planned to move to the $800 figure, and he encouraged immediate movement if at all possible. In response to these suggestions, the Employer representative disclosed that the Employer committee was prepared to move to the $800 figure. These efforts on the part of the Mediator produced a disclosure about the Employer's secret heart, which was highly critical to resolution of the first-year base rate. Such disclosures are essential to the mediator's role as a "third negotiator."

19. The Mediator as a "Third Negotiator— Neutral, but Not Neutered"

After assessing each party's pressure points and working to discover each party's secret heart, the mediator may begin to act openly as an additional negotiator, advocating on behalf of a possible basis for settlement.

This, of course, requires the mediator to identify a possible basis for settlement of disputed issues. Identifying a possible basis for settlement of disputed issues is one of the most challenging aspects of effective mediation. Indeed, some authors advise mediators to refrain altogether from trying to persuade parties that a particular settlement is advisable, simply because selecting the goal to be advocated is so difficult. They urge that the mediator's own preferences and sense of fairness will invariably affect how the target settlement is selected and that one person's sense of fairness should not be imposed on negotiating parties.

These commentators are quite right to criticize mediators who impose their preferences upon the parties. A mediator, unlike an arbitrator, should not impose his or her judgment about what constitutes a fair outcome on the parties. When parties employ an arbitrator, they ask that person to impose his or her judgment upon the parties and end their dispute. Parties employing a mediator, however, have *not* asked to have someone else's judgment imposed upon them. They have asked for help in finding their own, mutually acceptable solution.

Commentators are wrong, however, to suggest avoidance of this problem requires mediators to refrain altogether from pushing the parties toward a possible basis for settlement. Many disputes *cannot* be solved through any other means. The Case Study illustrates that after exposing the issues and seeking creative solutions, the parties may still remain opposed. Most of the economic issues in the Case Study displayed such opposition, and effective mediation demanded that something more be done.

Mediators can guard against imposing their preferences on the parties without resorting to sitting on their own hands. The key is *how* a possible basis for settlement is selected. It should not be grabbed out of the air nor should it simply be whatever strikes the mediator as fair.

The mediator must use experience and study to forecast where the relative bargaining strength of the parties would take them if they had all the time in the world to barter and work on effective communication. A mediator should be able to paint that picture for the parties much sooner than they themselves could enact it. Doing so holds the promise of saving the parties from wasted time and energy as well as the risk of hostile exchanges blocking any settlement.

An important caveat is necessary. When assessing each party's bargaining strength, the mediator must *not* simply accept hard-line positions that have been stated in an effort to gain an advantage in negotiations. The mediator must use the pressure points discussed in Section C(17) to make certain that displays of strength are realistic. The mediator must press the parties to recognize how viable their alternatives are to a negotiated deal. The parties must also be pressed to consider common concerns (i.e., the desirability of future business dealings or the welfare of a child) that ought to temper everyone's demands.

These steps will move the parties closer to their secret hearts (Section C(18)), and confidential inquiries should tell the mediator even more about the parties' actual expectations. With this information, the mediator may forecast where the relative bargaining strength of the parties would take them if they had all the time in the world to work on their problem. It is then time to begin actively moving both parties toward that goal, so they can achieve it with less wasted motion.

Dissecting the Case Study   141

Three issues from the Case Study illustrate in particular this aspect of a mediator's work. The first issue concerned the weekly base rate for the first year of the agreement just discussed in Section C(18). By the middle of Day 6, the Mediator had formed a clear view about a possible basis for settling this issue. The events that produced that view tell a great deal about his thought process. On Day 4, the parties exchanged a number of proposals which included a figure for the weekly base rate in the first year of the agreement. The Union's position fluctuated greatly. Its final position included a figure of $965. The Employer's proposals on Day 4 showed steady, though small, movement with reference to this issue. The Employer's proposal of 2:30 P.M. suggested a figure of $785. The Employer's final proposal of the day, communicated at 3:30 P.M., suggested a figure of $795.

On Day 5 the members of the Union committee participated in a membership meeting in which the status of the negotiations was discussed and reviewed. Because this meeting could be expected to affect the Union's position, the Mediator began Day 6 by encouraging the Union to prepare a new, comprehensive economic proposal. The Union committee accepted the Mediator's encouragement and spent most of the morning working on this project. The result was a comprehensive Union proposal, delivered at 11:30 A.M., which suggested a weekly base rate of $810 for the first year of the agreement.

As soon as the Mediator saw this figure, he knew that agreement on the weekly base rate for the first year of the contract was possible. The Employer's last position had been $795. This demand from the Union was only $15 greater. He also knew, however, on the basis of experience, that this chance for agreement could be lost. The Union committee had moved a significant distance between the afternoon of Day 4 and midday on Day 6. In one step, it lowered its proposal $155. A negotiating party who makes such substantial movement is clearly inviting compromise and wants to see some movement in return. The Mediator had every reason to expect that some movement from the Employer could occur. The past history of the parties rendered it highly unlikely that the Employer had put forth all of the money in its pocket with a full week of negotiations still lying ahead before the Day 13 deadline. If the movement the Union was expecting from the Employer did not occur, the Union committee's great expectations could suddenly become great disappointment and hostility, which might impede all further efforts at settlement.

For these reasons, the Mediator concluded that settlement of this issue would require the Employer to spend slightly more than $795.

He expected that $800 would be a salable figure. He then began to actively persuade both sides to accept this as an appropriate outcome.

When the Employer committee gave the Mediator its next written proposal, no movement was displayed on the weekly base rate figure for the first year of the agreement. The Employer maintained its prior position of $795. The Mediator did not passively relay this position on to the Union. Instead, he spoke privately with the Employer spokesperson and actively encouraged the Employer committee to improve its offer to $800. The Mediator pointed out that the Union committee had made very substantial movement and that it expected some reciprocal compromise. He emphasized that the Employer's next step could either create positive momentum that would be helpful through the remainder of the mediation *or* inspire such indignation that all progress would be blocked. The Employer representative admitted that the Employer committee had planned to improve its offer for the first-year base rate at a much later time in the negotiations. In response to the Mediator's advice, however, it was increased to $800 at this time.

The Mediator then took that proposal to the Union committee where the Union representative expressed consternation that the Employer group had only improved its position by $5 rather than moving the full $15 necessary to reach the Union's proposed figure of $810. The Mediator knew, however, that the Union probably did not have a realistic expectation that its proposal would be accepted totally. He accurately informed the Union that he had worked diligently to push the Employer up to the figure of $800, and that the Union was seeing a figure it would not have seen until late in the negotiations had the Mediator not advocated for early movement. Ultimately, the Mediator was successful in convincing the Union to accept the $800 figure as well.

In all the decisions and actions described above, the Mediator was acting as a "third negotiator," advocating on behalf of a possible basis for settlement. He retained his neutrality, because he was not seeking to mold the settlement in order to satisfy any partisan interests. He was only trying to help the parties reach the outcome that their relative bargaining strength warranted, far more efficiently than they could have if left to their own devices. Their own past history would have led them to barter back and forth up until the Day 13 deadline. When working against a deadline of that sort, it can never be presumed that cool heads will facilitate a final resolution. There is always the danger that a position or the manner in which it is communicated will cause tempers to flare and, in this instance, an unnecessary strike might have resulted. The role of the Mediator as a third negotiator was, therefore, highly important.

The Mediator was active as a third negotiator when the parties returned to discussion of economic issues on Day 10. He knew that this was an extremely critical time. Significant positive momentum had been created through the settlement of all noneconomic issues. If that momentum was not maintained, however, the Day 13 deadline could easily arrive before any settlement was reached, potentially causing an unnecessary strike. For this reason, the Mediator chose *not* to act solely as a messenger, relaying positions of the parties.

Throughout the sessions, the Mediator was giving thought to the bottom line which would afford a possible basis for settling the economic issues. He had reached the conclusion that the wage package would need to reflect $30,000 of earnings for musicians by the conclusion of the contract's term. His reasons for isolating this figure as a possible basis for settlement are highly important. He did not pick the figure of $30,000 because it was personally appealing to him or because it is a neat, round figure.

The Mediator had been listening very carefully to all of the comments offered by the Union's spokesperson in support of its wage proposals. He heard demands for sums far in excess of $30,000. He also heard something more important. He heard the Union's spokesperson use the figure $30,000 as an example of a "livable" wage from the very first session forward. When the Union prepared its first comprehensive economic proposal for the mediation sessions on Day 4, the goal of $30,000 in total earnings again played prominently, which the Mediator noted upon his analysis of the proposal.

The Mediator found these observations significant for two equally important reasons. First, he found these indicators to be signals from the Union committee about the goal it needed to attain before it could enthusiastically recommend a settlement to the total membership of the Union for ratification. Secondly, the Mediator knew from his experience that if the figure of $30,000 was playing a prominent part in the Union representative's speeches to management, it was also playing a prominent part in his speeches to the membership. This meant that the goal of $30,000 had quite likely become set in the minds of the members and difficulty could be expected in securing ratification for any settlement failing to attain that goal. The membership had been primed to work for a $30,000 wage package as the central accomplishment of the current negotiations.

These observations led the Mediator to conclude that the Union committee would not endorse any proposed settlement unless the $30,000 goal was met sometime during the contract's term. He was quite certain that the Employer committee would not agree to the attainment of this figure in the first year of the agreement, because this would amount to a percentage increase in wages far exceeding anything prevalent in similar labor negotiations. He did not know, however, if the Employer could be persuaded to reach that goal by the last year of the agreement. He decided, therefore, to press the Employer committee at the very beginning of Day 10 in order to discover as much as possible about the Employer's secret heart.

The Mediator met privately with the Employer committee on the morning of Day 10. He explained his reasons for finding significance in the figure of $30,000. He strongly encouraged the Employer committee to prepare a new proposal reaching that figure by the last year of the agreement's term, if at all possible. The Employer representative was hesitant. In the past, the parties had dickered back and forth about wages up until the very last moment. In this instance, some time still remained before the Day 13 deadline, and the Employer representative feared that a cushion ought to be preserved. The Mediator knew, however, that neither party had been completely satisfied with their past mode of dealing. Dickering back and forth until the last minute created a great deal of uncertainty and raised the risk of an unnecessary strike. He therefore encouraged the Employer representative to clean its pockets slightly earlier. The trust which had been cultivated by this time and the success achieved in resolving other issues made him confident that he could persuade the Union committee it was seeing the Employer's best proposal now, even though time remained before the Day 13 deadline.

In response to this active persuasion from the Mediator, the Employer committee did prepare a proposal featuring total wages for tenured musicians of $30,000 in the third year of the agreement. This displayed extremely significant movement from the Employer. It had improved its proposal for the weekly base rate during the third year of the agreement from $900 per week to $920 per week. This was a greater change than the Employer had made at any prior time during the negotiations, and the Mediator knew the Employer was making a substantial concession, which would not have taken place at this time but for his encouragement.

Because of this knowledge, the Mediator actively encouraged the Union Committee to accept this proposal. The Mediator was appropriately convinced that he had cleaned the Employer's pockets of all money available for wages, and he sought to assure the Union committee that such was the case. Because of these accurate observations from the Mediator, the Union committee was ultimately able to accept the Employer's wage proposal. The only further change which occurred in the complete economic package was a change to the regular pension contribution rate in the third year of the agreement. Some form of adjustment had to be made on this issue since it was initially settled on the basis of a four-year agreement, but the parties shifted to consideration of a three-year agreement during their wage discussions. The Mediator had retained notes of all matters requiring further discussion before a full settlement could be declared, and he knew that this was an issue which would have to be discussed further.

The efforts of the Mediator as a third negotiator on Day 10 were highly important to the overall success of the mediation. If he had served only as a messenger, the Employer committee would not have changed its position so substantially at the beginning of that day. In all likelihood, the parties would have emulated their usual pattern of exchanging increasingly small concessions right up until the last moment, despite the fact that this bargaining pattern posed problems for both sides in light of the uncertainty created. On their own, the parties could not free themselves from this pattern of dealing because they feared it was necessary to secure the best possible deal. The Mediator spared them from this inefficiency and uncertainty by speeding their progress toward a possible basis for settlement which was, in fact, mutually acceptable. This was only possible because he became a third negotiator, advocating on behalf of a possible basis for settlement which he had identified.

On a third occasion during the Case Study when the Mediator was acting as a third negotiator, he displayed use of a technique which can have special utility when seeking to move parties toward a possible basis for settlement. This occurred during the Mediator's efforts to persuade the parties that the formula for computing the one-time supplemental retirement benefit should be 60 percent of weekly salary during the last year of service multiplied by total years of service up to a cap of 38 years. The Mediator's reasons for selecting this formula as a possible basis of settlement are discussed in Section C(15) above.

As the Mediator thought in advance about what strategy he would employ to move each party toward this formula, he concluded that special efforts would be needed to secure the necessary movement from the Union committee since it was being asked to move the

146 THE ANATOMY OF MEDIATION

furthest. It had begun with a proposed formula including a figure of 100 percent. By contrast, the Employer had begun with a proposed formula including a figure of 50 percent. Since the benefit involved was an added benefit above and beyond the Employer's usual obligation to make pension contributions, the Employer committee was highly resistant to spending much more than its original proposal had contemplated. The Mediator knew, therefore, that the issue could not be settled unless the Union committee could be persuaded to move more significantly than displayed in its prior proposals. As the discussions progressed, the Mediator was looking for some special means that could be used to accomplish the greater movement necessary from the Union committee.

The Mediator ultimately found a "pocket concession" that could be used to accomplish this. During the Mediator's meeting with the Employer committee at 4:30 P.M. on Day 3, the Employer communicated its willingness to make regular pension contributions on *total* earnings, including overtime and extra engagements. The Mediator saw this as a rather significant concession since members of this bargaining unit had historically performed a significant number of extra engagements. He immediately concluded that this significant concession might be just the enticement necessary in order to bring the Union down to a percentage figure in the above-described formula that would be mutually acceptable. He also knew, however, that discussions on that issue had not progressed sufficiently so that he could make a final push for the Union to bring its percentage demand downward as far as was necessary. For these reasons, he did not communicate the Employer's concession to the Union committee immediately.

The Union had not only proposed that contributions be made on total earnings, it had also proposed that the regular rate for contributions be increased from seven and one-half percent to eight and one-half percent. In the meeting with the Union committee at 5:00 P.M. on Day 3, the Mediator told the Union committee that he was encountering great resistance concerning both these demands. He further told them that he was not certain either could be accomplished. After making these statements, he encouraged the Union committee to think long and hard about which demand ought to be considered its highest priority.

This step in the Mediator's actions might seem risky to some. By this time, the Mediator knew that the Employer was willing to adjust contributions and make them on total earnings. One might ask, "If the Union now identified the other demand as its higher priority, where would this leave the Mediator?" In fact, however, this step taken by the Mediator was extremely well conceived. It created highly useful options, no matter what the Union's response might be.

If the Union responded by stating that securing contributions on total earnings was its highest priority, this statement would enable the Mediator to make more effective use of the concession he was keeping in his pocket. Such a statement from the Union would, in essence, put a high price tag on that concession. Through such a statement, the Union would be recognizing that the concession held in the Mediator's pocket was an important one for them, and they could be expected to give something substantial in return for it. When the Mediator found the time appropriate, he could then suggest that the "something substantial" they needed to give for it was a significant concession on the percentage figure being disputed in the formula.

Significant leverage would also be available to the Mediator even if the Union made the opposite election. There was an equal chance that it might respond to the Mediator's question by saying that it cared more about increasing the regular contribution rate from seven and one-half percent to eight and one-half percent. If the Union did this, then the Mediator would need to return to the Employer committee and counsel it regarding its outstanding positions. He would need to tell the Employer committee that it could accomplish much more by making an adjustment in the regular contribution rate than by changing to make contributions on total earnings. In essence, he would try to swap the concession being held in his pocket for one which would be more attractive to the Union. After accomplishing this, the Mediator could then proceed to use his new pocket concession to "buy" the movement needed from the Union in the percentage figure disputed within the formula for supplemental benefits.

As it happened, the Union saved the Mediator some amount of effort. It responded to this question by telling the Mediator that securing contributions on total earnings was its higher priority. A high valuation was thereby placed on this concession, which the Mediator was then holding in his pocket. In a discussion the Mediator had with the Union committee at 6:00 P.M. on Day 3, he began to make use of that concession. By then, he had used creativity to plant within the Employer's mind the notion of a formula multiplying 60 percent by 38 years of service. In this discussion with the Union committee, he encouraged the Union to make a commitment to that figure *if* contributions on total earnings could be secured as a price for this concession from the Union. In response to the Mediator's encouragement, the Union agreed that this would be an appropriate exchange. At this juncture, the Mediator knew that he had the parties on the road to a settlement of pension issues, because he was already holding within his pocket the concession needed to accomplish the proposed exchange.

Certain cautionary observations should be made about the use of a pocket concession. It was highly useful to the Mediator in this circumstance as a critical device for his activities as a third negotiator, advocating on behalf of a possible basis for settlement. It should not be used indiscriminately, however. The Mediator used it here after reaching two conclusions that suggested it might have utility. First, he formed an impression about a possible basis for settlement concerning the formula in dispute. Secondly, he formed an impression as to which of the two parties would have to adjust their position most significantly in order to reach that possible basis for settlement. It was only after he determined that more movement would have to be secured from the Union, that he began keeping his eye peeled for some concession that might be withheld for the purpose of inspiring that necessary movement at a critical juncture. These characteristics made that tool a useful one to the Mediator in his role as a third negotiator.

Each of the three examples discussed above makes clear that the Mediator's actions as a third negotiator were critical to the effectiveness of the mediation portrayed in the Case Study. At this juncture, it is important to include comment on some concerns which others have raised about a mediator's role as a third negotiator, advocating for particular solutions.

Some authors express concern as to whether mediation is suited for all kinds of problems if the mediator adopts the role of a third negotiator as illustrated here. This concern is rooted in the method used to determine a possible basis for settlement. As explained here, that goal should be established by measuring the actual bargaining strengths of the parties, after they are tested through use of pressure points. Section C(17) explains that the alternatives the parties face if they do not settle are a key source of pressure points. If the problem would be subject to litigation, then the result which can be expected from the courts clearly has relevance.

It is in this situation that the problem identified by some authors becomes apparent. Sometimes plaintiffs do not rest their claims on *any* rights currently recognized by the courts. They file a lawsuit because they want to establish new rights under law. The case of *Brown v. Board of Education** is an example with which most people are familiar. Cases preceding the Supreme Court's decision in that matter allowed segregated schools, and the plaintiffs in *Brown* sought to establish for the first time that separate is not equal as far as education is concerned. If a mediator working with this kind of dispute thinks only about the current law when formulating pressure points, then this mediator may pressure the plaintiff to back down because, according to current law, no favorable result may be expected from a court. This has led some to advise that mediation is not a good process for resolving disputes in which claimants seek to have new rights recognized for the first time.

In fact, this supposed weakness in mediation becomes a significant strength *if* the mediator works to develop a more in-depth understanding of the pressure points. The truth of this statement is most evident if an example is considered. The circumstances are as follows:

> A tenant resides in a first floor apartment in the corner of a building which is located at an intersection in a residential neighborhood. Outside the tenant's living room window are approximately 12 feet of lawn bordered by a sidewalk. A bus stop is situated on the other side of the sidewalk. Because this is a heavily used bus stop, people frequently stand there. Many of them are teenagers on their way to school who congregate on the lawn and lean against the building nearby the tenant's living room window. The tenant is extremely concerned about the resulting noise and loss of privacy. The tenant has brought a claim asking that the landlord be required to construct a fence that will keep bus patrons off the lawn. The legal cases which have been decided in the state where these parties find themselves do not support the contention that landlords have a legal obligation to construct fences in these circumstances.

If a mediator faced with this circumstance thought only of the outcome which could be expected in court when identifying possible pressure points, that mediator could easily be led to lean more heavily on the tenant than the landlord in seeking to resolve this problem. That, however, would be a shallow and inadequate approach. There are pressure points, apart from the outcome to be expected from a court, which exist and which should be brought to bear upon the landlord's position in this dispute.

---

*347 U.S. 483 (1954).

If the landlord fails to resolve this problem, his alternative includes more than simply the prospect of a favorable court decision. The future, presuming no mutually satisfactory resolution, includes other features, and all are not favorable to the landlord. If people are congregating on the landlord's lawn and leaning against the landlord's building, it is highly likely that some damage is taking place. This damage is a cost to the landlord, and the mediator ought to make it a pressure point upon the landlord when considering whether some change of position would be advisable. The landlord is likely to face even greater costs, which are an available source of pressure points. If this tenant remains unhappy, he or she has one clear alternative to court litigation which may be pursued. The tenant may move at the conclusion of the lease, and if the same unattractive conditions which are causing this tenant to be unhappy present a perennial problem, the result may be frequent turnover in the occupancy of the apartment. Unless there is an extreme housing shortage in the area, this problem will most assuredly cost the landlord significant sums. Each time a tenant leaves, the landlord must go without rent until a replacement tenant is found. In this circumstance, there is a strong likelihood that investigation of the facts by the mediator would disclose that the landlord has encountered such problems in the past.

When all of these costs are considered, and brought to bear upon the landlord as pressure points, the alternative of building a fence of some sort may become the best possible basis for settlement. A fence may cost significantly less than the total package of expenses the landlord faces through refusal to deal with the problem, even though there may be no legal obligation to do so. The critical point here is that the outcome which might be expected from a court should never be the sole source of pressure points. In most circumstances, if a claim remains completely unresolved, the party who has responded to that claim will continue to face similar problems posing perennial costs. These facts need to be brought to bear in formulating the pressure points that the mediator may use in guiding the parties to a mutually acceptable resolution of their problems.

Certainly, in some circumstances, litigation must be pursued to conclusion in order to establish new rulings concerning the rights and responsibilities by which our society is governed. One should never presume, however, that a problem is not suited for mediation simply because one party has no solid case under the law as it stands. There may, nonetheless, be a mutually acceptable solution which is far preferable to the particular parties involved than the costs of litigation and the costs associated with failure to address the underlying problem.

20. When to Talk and When Not to Talk

The foregoing section portrays an aspect of effective mediation which requires very active efforts at persuasion. To keep these observations in perspective, however, it must be noted that the ability to remain silent is an equal, if not greater, asset for effective mediation. In the Case Study, before the Mediator began any efforts as a third negotiator, he patiently and quietly listened to the parties expound upon their views. He did this for several important reasons.

First, he knew from experience that people cannot be expected to accept advice about a possible basis for settlement unless they feel they have been "heard out" concerning the sources of dispute. The Mediator had a more important reason for listening, however, than simply appeasing everyone. He needed to listen carefully in order to find signals to be considered in formulating the possible bases for resolving various of the contested issues. Careful listening led the Mediator to forecast accurately that the Union committee required a wage package reaching $30,000 before the end of the agreement before it would enthusiastically recommend ratification to the membership.

There is an additional benefit to careful listening which should not be forgotten. Sometimes exhaustive use of all techniques summarized thus far in Chapter 2 can leave the parties some distance apart. It might appear in this instance that there is no alternative but to declare a hiatus in discussions. If there is reason to think that both sides have a strong desire for settlement, however, it can be productive simply to keep them in one place talking to each other. In the course of those discussions some germ of a new idea may appear. Even if no new idea emerges, one side or the other may become willing to express a possible concession on a test basis simply to see whether the reaction is sufficiently positive to warrant continuing work. In short, sometimes the best thing a mediator can do is nothing at all— nothing, that is, other than encouraging the parties to continue talking to one another in the hope that something will emerge which can be the basis for further progress. The discussion between the Mediator and the Observer which took place at 11:00 A.M. on Day 3 makes clear that this approach can produce significant progress.

21. Timing—How Are These All-Important Decisions Made?

The Introduction states that making decisions about timing is the most challenging aspect of mediation. Employing a given strategy at one time may produce failure, while employing it at another will produce success. Each of the foregoing sections in this Chapter comments not only about what the Mediator did but, more importantly, about what circumstances caused him to proceed in that fashion at a given time. These observations about timing are the most important commentary about each of the strategies discussed here, and they are also the most important source of information about timing decisions.

Some general observations concerning timing can be made at this juncture, however. The techniques discussed in Section B(11) (Peeling the Artichoke) and Section C(15) (Creativity) should always be employed before the mediator begins to work actively as a third negotiator. These two techniques can lead to win–win solutions. They can also lead to resolutions which do not require either side to make a concession, because some means is found to address current problems which creates no adverse consequences. Since these techniques can lead to this desirable outcome, they ought to be first choices before the mediation proceeds to resolutions requiring the parties to make concessions.

This advice is consistent with previous comments about what is necessary for a mediator to operate effectively as a third negotiator. It is clear that a mediator cannot be an effective third negotiator without investing considerable time listening carefully in order to identify a possible basis for settlement and considerable time cultivating trust so that efforts at persuasion will be well received. Thus, the mediator's role as an active third negotiator belongs at the later stages of a mediation.

Most timing decisions, however, cannot be made according to any hard and fast rules. Timing decisions are essentially necessary in order to mold the mediation process to the parties participating in any particular mediation. For this reason, one thing and one thing alone must be the paramount consideration in making timing decisions— the behavior of the parties. An effective mediator must pay very close attention to the signals displayed by behavior of participants to a mediation. For example, if participants to a mediation voice great confidence in the process, then a mediator may capitalize upon that momentum by tackling the most difficult issues first. By contrast, if participants to a mediation are suspicious or insecure concerning its benefits, then particular time must be taken to build confidence. In this circumstance, it makes more sense to begin with small, manageable issues where there is a high likelihood of resolution. Each time a choice is necessary, an effective mediator must pay similar heed to the behavior of the parties.

One of the central benefits mediation has to offer is the mediator's ability to customize both the process and the solution to accommodate the particular needs of the participants. This can only happen, however, if the mediator makes it happen by paying close attention to the needs of the parties, as displayed through their comments and actions.

22. *Alternatives to Mediation—Do They Play a Role?*

In the first joint session with the parties in the Case Study, the Mediator took time to explain the characteristics of mediation and how it differs from other processes for dispute resolution. This information is summarized in Chapter 4. Sometimes this step is necessary solely to make certain that all participants truly understand the extent of the commitment they have made by agreeing to participate in mediation. They have not agreed to let anyone else determine how their problems should be solved, but they have agreed to work diligently toward a mutually acceptable solution.

In this circumstance, the Mediator did not need to describe alternative processes for resolving disputes in order to accomplish this purpose. All of the participants were familiar with collective bargaining and the use of mediation in that setting. He had a second, important purpose for beginning the first joint session by recalling these alternatives for the parties. He knew that on some occasions parties to a dispute will share a strong desire to avoid costly alternatives to a settlement. Despite this strong desire, however, one or a few issues will remain at impasse, even after the fullest efforts at mediation. Since a mediator may not dictate a solution to the parties and impose it upon them, parties in this circumstance still face the prospect of a work stoppage, if the dispute has arisen between labor and management. If it has arisen elsewhere, some other equally undesirable alternative may face the parties.

In order to avoid an alternative everyone finds undesirable, it may become preferable to the parties to resolve one or a few issues by some means other than mediation. If they have resolved most areas of conflict through agreement, they may become willing to submit one or a few issues to some neutral individual such as an arbitrator. Since an arbitrator may impose an outcome on the parties, this process enables resolution of all conflicts without resort to a strike or other unattractive alternative. In short, the parties need to be reminded of the alternatives to mediation at the beginning of the process because one of those alternatives may become essential to the total resolution of their conflict.

D. Finalizing the Deal

The goal of mediation is to put an end to a given conflict. This means that the mediation may not stop simply because parties have voiced agreement about how their conflict should be resolved. Further steps must be taken in order to assure that agreements voiced become agreements which the parties live under peaceably.

23. *Suggesting Wording of Proposals for Clarity and Salability*

Sometimes parties will agree about what should happen in the future but will be incapable of expressing their agreement in clear language. This may be true because of inexperience with drafting, or simply because the heated nature of discussions has made each party unwilling to accept the other's language.

When such a circumstance exists, the mediator should not hesitate to propose specific language embodying the agreements expressed by the parties about what should take place in the future. The Mediator in the Case Study did this when the parties could not state their agreement concerning future negotiation of retiree fringe benefits. The Union had begun by proposing language that would make retirees a continuing part of the bargaining unit. The Employer committee expressed fear that this language would make retirees eligible to participate in ratification votes. It did not want that to happen. When this was communicated to the Union committee, they stated that they had no intention to allow participation of retirees in future ratification votes. This being the only concern of the Employer, there ultimately was no conflict between the parties. Nonetheless, they could not express their agreement in specific terms. The Employer wanted the Union to modify its original language, but the Union saw no need to do so.

The Mediator did not hesitate. He suggested that the parties embody their agreement with the sentence, "The issues affecting retirees are negotiable subjects in subsequent agreements."

Some mediators are hesitant to offer specific language. This hesitance is largely the product of unwarranted insecurity. Mediators sometimes fear that if disputes arise later about the meaning of language they have proposed that this will reflect unfavorably on the mediation process. Inaction is not the preferable solution for this problem, however. It is preferable to solve this problem by making certain that the meaning of all proposed language is discussed fully during the course of mediation so that no confusion will subsequently arise.

If language is first proposed while using shuttle diplomacy, this discussion should be held in the joint session conducted for the purpose of confirming in writing all agreements reached. The Mediator in the Case Study conducted such a session as soon as all issues relevant to retirees were settled. During such a session, each party may be asked to state at the bargaining table its understanding of language which has been initially proposed by the mediator. Of course, further work will be necessary if the statements of the parties are not in accord. Where they are in accord, that accord of the parties will be the basis for future construction of the language.

24. Prompt Drafting of the Settlement

Section C(14) above emphasizes that it is important for the mediator to assure agreements reached on discrete issues within a dispute are immediately recorded in writing. It is likewise important that the full settlement finally accomplished be completely drafted as quickly as possible. Even a short delay can cause the parties to begin recalling their agreements differently, thereby creating new conflict.

In the Case Study, the Mediator took steps to make certain that a complete settlement was drafted and available before the Union conducted its ratification vote. This pattern should be emulated in all mediations. Even though one party may not be facing a ratification vote, there is an equal potential for the parties to begin recalling their agreements differently, thereby creating problems. Prompt drafting is, therefore, always important.

25. Enforcement of the Settlement

Parties who have just reached a resolution of their conflicts are generally in a very upbeat, positive mood. They are not giving thought to any future disputes that could arise between the same parties. It is part of a mediator's job to keep the parties mindful of certain things they should do at this juncture in order to avoid future controversy or disputes.

Frequently, questions arise about the precise meaning of the settlement or about whether one party is complying with the settlement. Sometimes this happens because the parties walked away from the bargaining table with conflicting understandings about their agreement, and sometimes it happens because an unforeseen circumstance arises. The disruption created by these subsequent questions can be greatly diminished if the parties have agreed in advance as to how disputes over the meaning of their agreement will be resolved.

This is not generally a topic which needs to be expressly discussed in collective bargaining negotiations. If the parties have had an ongoing relationship, it is quite likely that their collective bargaining agreement will contain a provision requiring them to arbitrate questions of this kind. In other circumstances, however, the parties may not have an established means of dealing with such questions. If no private agreement has been made, disputes about an agreement are left for resolution in the courts.

This may not be desirable for two parties who have resolved an area of conflict through mediation. A desire to avoid court proceedings may have played very substantially in the decisions of those parties to utilize mediation in the first place. If future court litigation is not desirable, then the parties need to think about what private agreement should be included in their current settlement so as to provide a means for resolving future questions over the meaning of the settlement.

If this topic does not occur to the parties themselves, the mediator should direct attention to it. All of the alternative means for resolving disputes discussed in Chapter 4 are available for use in resolving questions that can arise about the meaning of a settlement reached in mediation. The mediator may advise the parties about the characteristics of each approach and which might be most desirable in their circumstance. The central asset of arbitration is that it provides a binding determination which is enforceable in court without detailed review. This assures that disputes about the meaning of a mediated settlement will not persist, nor will they create problems for an undue length of time.

Giving some small thought to this topic before a mediation is concluded can do a great deal to minimize the extent to which conflict and disruption are experienced by the parties to a mediation in the future.

E. Conclusion

This summary omits one added ingredient which is essential for effective mediation—EFFORT. If a mediator is content with "some progress," even though a full settlement is not attained, then "some progress" is all that will ever occur. The goal of a full settlement must be kept paramount in order to maintain the energy essential to use of the skills and techniques displayed in the Case Study.

This review of those skills and techniques makes clear that they are far more than tools helpful to the resolution of labor disputes. When combined with the requisite effort, they are key ingredients which can make mediation an effective means for the resolution of all problems: commercial disputes, family problems, neighborhood problems, environmental problems, indeed, most disputes in which human beings are participants. Chapter 3 displays how the application of these techniques to a variety of such issues may hold the key to effective mediation.

Chapter 3

Application to Varied Settings

Each of the situations described in this Chapter is representative of the disputes that arise concerning a particular type of subject. Following each situation description is a discussion explaining how the techniques demonstrated in the Case Study could be used to *begin* successful mediation of the problem.

The appropriate strategy once progress was accomplished would, of course, depend on the nature of the developments occurring in the mediation. Some of the situations pose problems which would require extensive effort by a skilled mediator in order to fully implement the recommended mediation strategy.

The intent here is only to provide an outline of the techniques most pertinent to the problem. The number references in the headings that are part of the recommended mediation strategy are those used previously throughout the book when each topic has been discussed.

Situation No. 1
A Complex Business Dispute

NASA awarded contracts for the construction of a complex satellite communications system to two companies, at a time when the system was not yet fully designed. While the project was developing, NASA gave directions to the companies that included various technical requirements. The companies took the position that these technical requirements were changes in the original contract entitling them to additional compensation. NASA took the position that the services required by the directions were contemplated as part of the original contract price.

All three parties, the two companies and NASA, sought mediation before resorting to any litigation in the hope of avoiding the extremely high litigation costs that would be involved in the preparation and presentation of this complex and technical dispute. They will be assisted in the mediation by the counsel who would represent them in the event of a lawsuit.

The Mediation Strategy

(9) *The Order of Attack*

As the Case Study makes clear, no formal rules exist controlling the mediation process, requiring joint meetings at a particular time or other forms of communication at other times. The mediator has responsibility for establishing the order of attack, as guided by the needs of the parties and the nature of the dispute. The decisions a mediator makes about the order of attack are highly important because failure to proceed effectively at early stages of the process can destroy the confidence and optimism parties generally bring to the process, and substantially diminish chances for success.

For these reasons, when a mediator faces a complex case, it is particularly important to give careful thought to the proper order of attack before convening formal sessions attended by all parties.

(10) *What Are the Issues as the Parties See Them?*

The mediator will be aided in establishing an effective order of attack in a case such as this if he or she begins by requesting all parties to submit a very *brief* written statement summarizing the background concerning the dispute as perceived by that party and the contentions made thus far by that party. In requesting such a statement, it is important for the mediator to emphasize that the document should not be prepared in the same fashion as a memorandum to a court of law. In that circumstance, counsel would support all positions with lengthy argument. Such argument would not be helpful at this stage, and indeed could be harmful. Reading such argument has a tendency to heighten the ardor of clients and cause them to be more resolved about positions previously taken. The mediator should carefully explain to each party when requesting these submissions, therefore, that the goal is clear identification of the issues in dispute, *not* preparation of a complete defense for each parties' position.

In a case such as this, it is highly likely that statements submitted by the parties would display some need for facts to be established concerning the various technical issues in dispute. Questions would likely arise such as: Have the parties performed similar contracts in the past? If so, what technical requirements have been treated as encompassed within the original contract price? Was this project less fully designed than others when the contract was awarded? If so, what information was communicated about completion of the design and technical refinements required thereby? Additional questions would doubtless arise, depending upon the precise controversy.

(12) Pressing for Known and Discovering Unkown Facts

If the written statements of the parties disclosed a need to establish facts, as just suggested, then the mediator would need to develop a plan for bringing the parties to a mutual understanding of those facts as efficiently as possible. Because of the complexity of this case, it may not be presumed that bringing the parties together for a joint meeting and directing their attention to discussion of the facts would likely be efficient. There is too great a danger that all parties would not bring all necessary documents to that session nor all persons with the requisite technical knowledge on particular points. For these reasons, it will likely be more efficient if the mediator brings counsel for all parties together in a preliminary joint session for the express purpose of discussing what information ought to be exchanged before direct efforts are made at settlement. Counsel may be encouraged to bring "wish lists" to such a joint meeting, reflecting all of the documents that they would like to see before making direct efforts at settlement. These "wish lists" might include summaries of information which could be given by various persons if they were serving as witnesses. The mediator may then operate from these lists to determine what information needs to be exchanged and viewed by everyone, including the mediator, in order to facilitate a common understanding of the facts.

A step such as this is most likely to be necessary in a complex case where mediation is sought before initiation of any litigation, in the hope of avoiding all litigation costs. In such a circumstance, the parties will have exchanged very little information, and some exchange of information is necessary before direct efforts may be made at settlement. If that exchange is accomplished through this format, however, rather than through the very specific rules of discovery that would control a court case, the mediator can supervise and make certain that everything occurs according to a compact schedule and that the parties focus upon items of importance.

By the conclusion of this joint session, the mediator should bring the parties to a specific agreement upon a schedule for completing the exchange of information and a schedule for future sessions. The mediator must then oversee any exchange of information agreed upon in order to assure that disputes do not arise and delays do not occur.

(17) What Are Each Party's Pressure Points?

While information is being exchanged and assessed by the mediator, the mediator will clearly be reaching some tentative conclusions about the issues in dispute. It is equally important that the mediator begin to assess seriously each party's pressure points. What factors should induce each party to make concessions toward a mutually acceptable resolution? In most business disputes, a variety of such pressure points will exist. Here, the parties have already expressed their collective desire to avoid the high cost of litigating a technical dispute of this kind. Careful consideration of the parties' circumstances also discloses additional pressure points. These are parties which all have a desire to continue working with one another. The contracting companies doubtless have a desire to receive further contracts from NASA in the future. Likewise, NASA should be interested in retaining the interest of these contracting companies since its purposes are favored by maintaining a qualified, interested pool of contractors available to bid on future projects. This desire of all parties to work with one another in the future may be brought to bear by the mediator as a pressure point, suggesting that all parties ought to make themselves open to any reasonable resolution put forth. In other business disputes, the desire to avoid adverse publicity, or take advantage of a customized resolution which could not be secured from a court, may supply the pressure points necessary for the mediator's future work.

(1) Are All "Parties" Present at the Mediation Sessions?

After the mediator has supervised exchange of information about controlling facts, and given preliminary thought to the pressure points that may be used to resolve the dispute, it will be time to direct the parties' efforts toward settlement. When convening a joint meeting for this purpose, the mediator should take steps to be certain that top management personnel, who have authority to make final decisions, attend on behalf of all parties. At this and future sessions, the mediator will be suggesting that the mutually discovered facts and pressure points warrant resolution of the dispute. It will be pointless to address these matters unless those persons are present who can assess what is said and make a commitment. No one should need to make telephone calls and translate events at the mediation in an effort to persuade some absent decision-maker that a concession is warranted.

With top management from all parties present, it will be helpful to begin by allowing each party to explain fully the positions it has previously adopted, and what it has learned through the exchange of information supervised by the mediator. This step is generally very important for adjusting the perspectives of the top management representatives present. Previously, each will have only heard a favorable recitation of the facts, given by their own support personnel. This facet of the mediation, however, will expose them most clearly to all unfavorable facts, which may warrant an adjustment in positions previously taken. The mediator may specify that each party will be given a certain period of time to make its uninterrupted presentation in order to make certain that the presentations remain focused and the attention of the top management representatives attending is maintained.

(21) Timing—How Are These All-Important Decisions Made?

After the step described above is taken, according to a schedule determined by the mediator, the next order of attack will have to be selected, according to the "signals" displayed by top management representatives thus far. If all parties continue to display intransigence, then the mediator will need to speak with each party separately in order to talk persuasively about what has been said and explain why it should evoke a change in position. On the other hand, if top management seem favorably impressed by what they have heard from other parties, then it will likely be useful to convene a meeting with the mediator and the top management representative from each party, in order to address the problem collectively and collaboratively seek a solution. In such a session, the mediator will need to make use of the pressure points which have been identified in order to remind everyone that a negotiated solution is preferable to the alternatives facing the parties.

The factual description for this scenario was drawn from an actual dispute which arose between NASA, TRW, Inc., and SpaceCom. In that circumstance, the contractors filed the claim with the NASA Board of Contract Appeals. They engaged in a full year of active discovery and other pre-hearing preparation. Thereafter, they used a form of minitrial (see Chapter 4) in which all parties made 2½-hour presentations before top management representatives. No neutral panel member was selected. After this session, the top management representatives were able to reach a settlement after meetings on two separate days. There is, therefore, every reason to believe that the steps described here may efficiently produce resolution of a complex, technical dispute.

The minitrial procedure accomplished considerable efficiency for these parties. For other parties, the mediation process might be a more useful and efficient device. For example, when mediation is sought before litigation is commenced, the mediator's supervised exchange of information may take the place of formal discovery, which is likely to be far more costly and time consuming. In the actual dispute between NASA, TRW Inc., and SpaceCom, the parties spent a full year engaged in active discovery. Additionally, other parties may find it useful if a single, neutral person with the requisite expertise is involved in their settlement efforts, so that reticent parties can be reminded of pressure points which ought to adjust their positions at appropriate times. This can be accomplished either through mediation, or through inclusion of a neutral member on the minitrial panel, since such neutral members perform many of the same functions as mediators.

Situation No. 2
A Sex Harassment Claim

The plaintiff was employed as an assistant administrator at a hospital which is part of a nationwide enterprise operating hospitals for profit. Three months ago she resigned her employment. Shortly thereafter, she retained a lawyer who sent the hospital a demand letter.

It asserted that for four years the hospital administrator had created a sexually hostile work environment; that he repeatedly asked the plaintiff to have cocktails or dinner with him, although she did not desire to do so; that on some occasions, the plaintiff felt compelled to accept these invitations because the administrator was her supervisor; that the administrator constantly made sexually suggestive remarks which were unwelcome; that the plaintiff never responded in kind; that the administrator frequently put his hand around the plaintiff's waist, and thereafter began to let it slide down to her buttocks; that the plaintiff always abruptly removed the administrator's hand; that, three months before she left employment, this hostile work environment became intolerable when the administrator stated to the plaintiff, "why don't you just get into my pants where you've always wanted to be?"; that this statement was made in a room where a secretary was present; that this left the plaintiff with no alternative but to leave her employment; and, that her resignation was therefore really a constructive discharge.

At the suggestion of their attorneys, both the hospital and the plaintiff have agreed to attempt mediation before any litigation is initiated. Private conversations between the mediator and counsel indicate that the hospital was principally motivated by a desire to avoid adverse publicity and the plaintiff was primarily motivated by a desire to avoid the emotional challenge litigation would present. The lawyers will participate in the mediation as spokespersons, when appropriate, and advisers to their clients.

The Mediation Strategy

(21) Timing—How Are These All-Important Decisions Made?

Some lawyers might question the wisdom of using mediation at this time, before any lawsuit is on file and before each side has used the formal discovery process of litigation to search for helpful information. Unquestionably, some facts must be investigated before a lawyer can give reliable advice to a client about whether any particular settlement compares favorably to the outcome which could be expected before a court.

In many cases, however, the relevant facts may be investigated without the heavy cost that formal discovery imposes. As will be seen from the developments discussed hereafter, these lawyers wisely determined that the costs to their clients could be minimized by pursuing mediation at this time.

If mediation is sought before all the relevant facts have been investigated, then it is part of the mediator's job to supervise efficient investigation of the facts, as was done in Situation No. 1.

Application to Varied Settings 165

(4) Joint Meetings Versus "Shuttle Diplomacy"

(9) **The Order of Attack**

Chapter 2 explains that generally it makes sense for a mediation to begin with a joint meeting in which each party is given a full and uninterrupted opportunity to explain its views about the dispute. The observation is made there that frequently each party hears more and learns more than they have previously through this device because they are required to listen patiently. This technique is successfully employed in Situation No. 3, which follows.

A mediator must remain sensitive, however, to special characteristics of a given dispute which indicate this general advice should not be taken. The present dispute is one in which several participants are likely to have very strong emotional reactions to one another. The plaintiff alleges that she left her employment because she could not abide the environment created by her superior. Since these are her contentions, she may not be prepared to attempt mediation in his presence. Likewise, it can be expected that the administrator, who is at the receiving end of these accusations, may have strong emotional reactions.

Some professionals will not attempt mediation unless the parties can be persuaded to meet jointly. Their view is that mediation should strive to open channels of communication and that this cannot happen if disputing parties are allowed to become dependent upon a go-between. This view warrants starting mediation with a joint session whenever possible. It does *not*, however, warrant the conclusion that mediation should never proceed in any other way for two reasons.

First, there is more than one possible route to the goal of enabling direct communication. Even though parties begin with such hostility that they are unwilling to be in the same room, shuttle diplomacy can change these attitudes. New information can be brought to bear changing perceptions or bringing into focus interests that warrant direct communication.

Second, while opening channels of communication is a positive goal for mediation, there is no reason to make it the exclusive goal of mediation. Some disputing parties have no continuing relationship and no need to deal with one another about anything other than a single claim. If they want to solve their current problem without working on direct communication, litigation need *not* be their only alternative. A skilled mediator may still help them to accept voluntarily a resolution that compares well with that alternative, *and* requires less time and expense.

The facts for this scenario indicate that both parties have strong reasons to avoid trial. They therefore have good reason to make use of mediation even though feelings might prevent them from beginning their efforts in joint session.

For these reasons, the mediator should discuss the order of attack with both counsel before any session commences. In this circumstance, it will be supposed that such consultation warrants keeping the parties in separate rooms and operating through shuttle diplomacy from the beginning of the mediation.

(7) Obtaining the Trust of the Parties

(12) Pressing for Known Facts and Discovering Unknown Facts

The mediator may feel that the plaintiff's demand letter states rather completely both the recollections and position of the plaintiff. Nonetheless, it will be extremely important during the first private session with the plaintiff to request a detailed narrative directly from her. This is true for two equally important reasons.

First, the mediator will need to ask questions of the plaintiff as she is telling her story. This may lead to discovery of certain facts which would make her case less than a clear winner if she were to take it to trial. The mediator needs to discover such facts in order to identify pressure points that should induce the plaintiff to lower her demands and accept something less than her greatest expectations as an appropriate resolution of the case. Hearing the story directly will also enable the mediator to speak knowledgeably to the hospital about the likelihood that the plaintiff would prevail at trial.

Some lawyers have reservations about using mediation because they do not want a mediator to ask questions that may cause a client to disclose weaknesses in their case. This attitude, however, is very short-sighted. If the problem is litigated, these weaknesses will eventually be disclosed. The system that occurs before and during American trials makes it impossible for such things to remain hidden forever. It is in the client's best interests, therefore, for everyone to become realistic as early as possible. This is essential to avoid very disappointing results later, and to develop a sound recognition for what might constitute a fair resolution now, before funds are unnecessarily spent on many hours of lawyers' work.

The mediator's second reason for listening carefully and completely to the plaintiff in this circumstance concerns the need to build trust. If the mediator does learn of information which warrants encouraging the plaintiff to reduce her demands, that encouragement will take place sometime during the mediation. When it does, the plaintiff will not respond well if she does not personally believe that the mediator listened carefully to her before reaching any conclusions about possible weaknesses in her case. Ample time should be invested at this stage, therefore, and the mediator should remain mindful that "you cannot eat a hot bun in one bite."

For purposes of further discussion here, we will suppose that the mediator learned several added pieces of important information by asking questions during the plaintiff's narrative. The mediator learned that according to the plaintiff, the secretary who was in the room during the administrator's alleged offensive remark immediately asked the plaintiff, "Why do you let men talk to you that way?" The mediator also learned, however, that the plaintiff's counsel has subsequently interviewed this secretary and that her recollection differs. During this interview, the secretary recalled that she was unable to hear precisely what was said between the administrator and the plaintiff because the words were spoken on the other side of the room. She did recall, however, that after this discussion, the plaintiff was extremely angry and approached the secretary immediately. She further recalled that the plaintiff was visibly distraught and crying; that the plaintiff asked her, "Did you hear what he said?" and, that the two of them spoke briefly.

Through additional questions, the mediator learned that the plaintiff had complained about this incident to another assistant administrator with greater responsibility than she had; that this individual told her to let him know if she had any further problems; that the administrator thereafter became very cold toward her; that she feared, in light of this, that her job would suffer during cutbacks planned over the next six months; and, that, in part, she resigned because she wanted to leave while her employment was in good standing rather than waiting to be laid off.

In this first session, the mediator requested a copy of the plaintiff's letter of resignation. The mediator saw that while it was two and one-half pages long, it did not make any reference to a sexually hostile work environment as one of the causes for her departure. It contained lengthy explanations of the reasons why the plaintiff felt that her wages were deficient for her responsibilities, and cited this as the central reason for resignation.

In the first private session with hospital management, the mediator would, of course, wish to ask similar questions in order to elicit management's understanding of the facts. For purposes of further discussion, we will suppose that the mediator's questions establish that the administrator denies having stated, "Why don't you just get into my pants where you've always wanted to be?" According to the administrator, shortly before this alleged incident occurred, he criticized the plaintiff for making a decision beyond her level of responsibility. He was angry with her at the time of the alleged comment, and he recalls having said, "Why don't you move into my office where you've always wanted to be?" The administrator further indicates that he did learn from the person to whom the plaintiff complained that she felt he had said something sexually offensive, and that in order to avoid any future miscommunication, he tried to say as little as possible to her thereafter.

(18) Discovering Each Party's "Secret Heart"

In the first private session with each party, the mediator needs to do something additional after pressing for known facts and discovering unknown facts. The mediator needs to conclude the first private session with the plaintiff by pressing to discover precisely what she hopes to secure for satisfaction of her claim. If the demand letter prepared by her attorney is typical, it will simply ask for a specified sum of money. A specified sum of money is not always, however, what is most important to a plaintiff such as this one. Many other objectives may be of equal or greater importance.

The plaintiff may feel injured, and may be strongly motivated by a desire to make certain that employer policies are changed so that no other employee suffers similar injury. Another goal is prevalent in employment cases of this type, and the mediator should ask specific questions to discover whether it is present in any particular case. If a dispute has caused an employee to leave employment, frequently that person's paramount goal will be resumption of good, acceptable employment. A sizable monetary settlement has some obvious appeal. Most people, however, do not find complete satisfaction in the promise of a single lump-sum settlement. Most people have a desire to be and remain productive.

For purposes of discussion here, we will presume that when pressed to disclose her "secret heart," the plaintiff listed several goals. She does feel injured and would like to be assured that no women who remain in employment at the hospital will be similarly injured. She also has a strong desire to remain productive and to have a good, secure job. She is adamant in stating that she is *not* interested in returning to work at the hospital. As yet, she has not felt able to seek employment actively in the same community, because she fears that most prospective employers in the medical field would know her former administrator and that she could not count upon him for a favorable recommendation.

The plaintiff also feels that she was forced to leave her employment, and that the hospital should therefore cover the expenses that she has had to pay during her period of unemployment thus far. Lastly, but not insignificantly, she feels a strong desire for retribution, and knows of no way to accomplish that other than through pressing for a monetary settlement that is large enough to get the hospital's attention.

At the conclusion of the mediator's first private session with the hospital representatives, questions need to be asked in order to discover which of these goals might most easily be met. First and foremost, the mediator should discover whether the hospital regarded the plaintiff as a good employee for whom enthusiastic recommendations could be prepared. If they can, then the mediator ought to encourage all persons present with knowledge of the plaintiff to begin drafting recommendation letters immediately which might be shown to her as an element of a full settlement. If the hospital and the administrator are positive about the plaintiff's work performance, then the mediator should also explore the nature of any contacts that the hospital could use to develop employment opportunities for the plaintiff.

At this time, the mediator may also ask whether the hospital has any new procedures or training to help management avoid the perception of a sexually hostile work environment. If it does, this may be useful in addressing the plaintiff's expressed concern over the conditions of other employees in the future.

(19) *The Mediator as a "Third Negotiator"*

If letters of recommendation are drafted, with input from the mediator to ensure they are as positive as possible, then they should promptly be shown to the plaintiff. This should persuade her that significant things can be secured from the mediation process, which will not be available to her if she presses her claim through litigation. Any new procedures or training discovered by the mediator may also be called to the plaintiff's attention.

Once both parties see that the mediation process can be beneficial to them, it is time for the mediator to begin working more actively as a third negotiator. The mediator should press both parties for a reasonable position concerning the economic aspect of a possible settlement. The initial positions expressed by both parties will likely be far apart. No purpose will be served by simply communicating these unacceptable offers back and forth and waiting for the parties to inch forward. Rather, the mediator should press each party to adjust its initial position closer to the bottom line contemplated within their "secret hearts" in order to avoid wasted motion.

In nearly all cases, even after the mediator has knowledge of the parties' "adjusted" positions, they will remain some distance apart. At this stage, the mediator should consider selecting a suggested basis for settlement which may be advanced to both sides as a recommendation from the mediator. Such a recommendation should not be generated simply by splitting the difference between the parties. That is something they could have accomplished on their own, without the assistance of a mediator, and there is, therefore, no persuasive reason for either party to accept such a figure.

Rather, the mediator should select a recommended settlement figure by assessing the alternative each party faces in court if they fail to settle. In this circumstance, the alternative of litigation is the primary source of pressure points. Both sides should be willing to settle if the agreed-upon settlement is more favorable than the alternative they face. The alternatives the mediator should assess here include the range of judgments such cases garner when fully litigated, the strengths and weaknesses of each side's factual case, and the independent reasons each party has for avoiding litigation. Here, those include not only the time and expense of litigation, but also the emotional demands that would be made on participants for both parties.

Once the mediator has selected such a recommended basis for settlement, it may be advanced to both sides individually, with a complete explanation of the reasons it should be adopted. In this circumstance, the mediator could and should focus attention of both parties on the factual weaknesses in their cases which the mediator discovered during the first private sessions.

Without criticizing the sincerity of the plaintiff's claim, the mediator may counsel her concerning certain factual flaws in her case that render the results she would obtain from litigation uncertain. It is not helpful that the principal witness to the worst of the comments she attributes to the administrator cannot corroborate her account in significant respects. The plaintiff thinks that the secretary immediately said something acknowledging that she heard the administrator's comment the same way, but the secretary will not support this. This inconsistency could be harmful to the plaintiff at trial. Likewise, the plaintiff's claim that she was coerced into leaving her employment because of a sexually hostile work environment is damaged by the fact that her lengthy letter of resignation cites different reasons. These facts, learned by the mediator, should be cited as reasons for a further adjustment, bringing the plaintiff to the figure selected by the mediator as a recommended basis for settlement.

The mediator has similar reasons for speaking persuasively to the hospital group. Although the plaintiff and the secretary recall the critical incident differently, the secretary's recollection could, nonetheless, be seen as strong support for the plaintiff's ultimate accusation that the words spoken by the administrator were, "Why don't you get into my pants where you've always wanted to be?" The secretary can verify that the plaintiff was immediately distraught by whatever she heard, and she was seemingly much more upset than one would be if their superior said, "Why don't you move into my office where you have always wanted to be?" These are considerations which could lead a jury to credit the plaintiff's recollections and find that the administrator did, in fact, make the comment alleged. No matter what verdict this may lead to, the hospital has clear reason for avoiding the adverse publicity which would ensue if its hospital administrator was found to have said such a thing. Such efforts on the part of the mediator should bring the parties' economic positions far closer than they have previously been, and potentially to the point of settlement. It may not, however, be possible to reach a full settlement before the plaintiff finds alternate employment. For understandable reasons, a plaintiff will seek far more money from settlement of a claim if that plaintiff fears indefinite unemployment than if the future is more secure because of a new job.

In this circumstance, some employers are hesitant to release letters of recommendation even though they are truthful, because they want to make the letters an enticement to enter into a full and complete settlement, through which the plaintiff resolves pending claims. If such a view is encountered in this circumstance, the mediator will need to speak forcefully and persuasively to the employer group, as a third negotiator. This possible employer view is a shortsighted one. The employer's interests are best served if the plaintiff resumes employment as quickly as possible. Not only will that minimize any damages that she might claim, but moreover, it will render the plaintiff financially secure and more likely to enter into a complete resolution of her claims. The mediator may need to persuade the employer of these facts in order to secure its assistance in the plaintiff's job search before a final resolution can be accomplished.

Situation No. 3
A Neighborhood Problem

Bill Ford and his family moved two months ago because of a corporate transfer. Since then they have been making diligent efforts to sell their home. After the Fords put the home on the market, two prospective purchasers were extremely interested, but balked just before the scheduled meeting for execution of formal papers. Because of their urgent interest in selling the property, the Fords reduced the price. Recently, Bob and Betty Brady appeared extremely interested in the home, but they backed out just before legally committing themselves as well.

Bob and Betty Brady informed Bill that they were set to buy until the immediate neighbor, Ethel Biden, strolled over to chat as they were recently inspecting the property. While that conversation was going on, Ethel said she wished to make certain the new occupants understood that the kitchen could not be used after 8:00 P.M. because it is only a few feet from her bedroom.

The Bradys told Bill that they did not want to walk into a new home with those sorts of "neighbor" problems. Bill asked the Bradys whether they would still be interested in the home if he could straighten things out with Mrs. Biden. Their reply was, "We like the house, but we don't want to buy any hassles. We'll keep looking, but feel free to call if you think you have her straightened out."

Bill was irate after his conversation with the Bradys. He called his real estate agent to see whether he could recommend an attorney that might be able to represent him in an action against Mrs. Biden. The real estate agent told Bill he might think about trying a new Neighborhood Mediation Center which had been getting attention in the local paper. Bill has furnished the Center with information about his problem.

The Mediation Strategy

(1) Are All Parties at the Mediation Session?

First, it will be essential for someone from the Mediation Center to approach Ethel and determine if she will be willing to participate in a mediation hearing.

There are good reasons why she should do so which may be called to her attention. Bill is irate and was on the verge of filing a lawsuit. Even if he has no valid claim against Ethel, that could end up costing her considerable money and inconvenience. She would need to retain a lawyer, and under the American system, she could expect to pay her own counsel fees even if she won. We may assume that these facts would convince Ethel to participate.

There are further parties missing at this stage. The possible purchasers, the Bradys, are actually the ones who expressed uncertainty about whether they could live happily next door to Ethel. It is highly unlikely, however, that they can be encouraged to participate. They backed out of the sale because they did not want to be troubled by dealings with Ethel. Bill would not want anyone to contact them because further "hassles" could destroy the tentative interest that they still have in the house.

As indicated in Chapter 2, when the participation of an interested party cannot be secured, the mediator(s) must take particular care to be certain that the concerns of that party are addressed so that the mediation will bring a true end to conflict. In this circumstance, that means that care will have to be taken to assure that the concerns of the Bradys are addressed, since they will not be there to address them.

(4) Joint Meetings

(12) Pressing for Known Facts

Neighborhood Mediation Centers of the sort described here frequently use a panel of mediators including trained volunteers from the community. Community members are found to have the requisite credibility and expertise concerning the kinds of problems that arise.

In this circumstance, the mediation panel would want to begin with a joint meeting in which both Bill and Ethel participated. This session could accomplish one of the central benefits of joint meetings discussed in Chapter 2. Frequently disputing parties do not understand one another's point of view because they have never listened to one another. If they each are required to sit patiently while the other explains their point of view to a mediator or mediation panel, things will be heard for the first time that may give new perspective.

The panel should assure that these full explanations take place by setting forth some ground rules at the beginning of the session. Among other things, they should explain that each person ought to refrain from interrupting while the other gives an initial explanation of their reasons for concern. Then the panel may ask Bill to explain fully why he believes there is a problem requiring attention. After he has finished, Ethel should be asked for her side of the story.

The possible benefits to be derived from these first steps should not be underestimated. Bill will explain that because the house has not sold, his family is making two mortgage payments each month, draining their resources by an extra $1000 per month or more. Ethel may not have had any idea how much economic loss her intervention was causing the Fords. While this alone may not persuade her to change her views, it will certainly affect her willingness to think about alternatives more satisfactory to everyone.

(11) Peeling the Artichoke—Finding the Heart of the Matter

After both Bill and Ethel have made complete initial statements, the mediation panel will need to ask questions in order to peel away the positions each person has adopted and find out more about the underlying circumstances that have produced a problem.

In this circumstance, it will be most important to ask Ethel what specific past problems have caused her to raise objection over use of the kitchen after 8:00 P.M. The further course of the mediation will be affected considerably by her response. One possible response will be suggested here to illustrate the further steps thereby made appropriate.

Ethel might respond by explaining that the dishwasher in the Fords' kitchen is so loud and runs so long that it has disturbed her sleep on past occasions when retiring at her regular hour of 9:00 P.M.

(21) Timing—How Are These All-Important Decisions Made

(20) When to Talk and When Not to Talk

Once this information has been brought out, the mediation will be at a critical stage. The mediators will probably be tempted to begin suggesting solutions to Bill and Ethel. Quiet dishwashers are available and they cost quite a bit less than a lawsuit would cost either of these parties.

As the discussion of timing in Chapter 2 makes clear, however, mediators should not suggest solutions until other techniques are tried first. If the parties find a solution themselves, they will be far happier with it and far more likely to live up to the deal they strike than if they feel something has been forced on them.

For these reasons, the mediators should ask questions to draw out each party's reaction to the new information which has emerged. This will give them a chance to fashion a solution if they are willing and able to do so.

If the parties show that they have been affected to some degree by hearing the other person's side of the story, then the mediators should not hesitate to allow a full exploratory discussion. This will be a good time "not to talk"—to afford the fullest opportunity for the parties to come up with possible solutions.

(19) The Mediator as a "Third Negotiator"

If one party or the other displays no recognition that compromise is better than the alternatives, then the mediation panel should remind that party of what reality holds in store. Suppose for example that Bill insists he has no legal obligation to make any changes for the purpose of accommodating Ethel. While Bill may have no legal obligation toward his neighbor to acquire the most quiet dishwasher possible, that small investment is far preferable to him in economic terms than the losses he is currently suffering. Because his neighbor is unhappy and disrupting sale of his home, Bill is currently required to cover two mortgage payments. The mediation panel should not hesitate to point these facts out to Bill.

(14) Converting "Agreements in Theory" to Agreements in Fact

If Bill becomes persuaded that it makes more sense to purchase a new dishwasher for the home than risk disruption of future sales, or some other solution is agreed upon by the parties, the mediation panel will still have some important work left to do. As noted above, the interests of the Bradys, who are not participating directly in the mediation, must be kept in mind.

The Bradys informed Bill that they would only resume the sales transaction if he succeeded in "straightening out" Ethel. Bill's problem will not be solved, therefore, unless the Bradys are given some showing that Ethel will no longer be raising objections about use of the kitchen. If Bill does not raise a concern about the need for this showing, the mediators should bring it up because failure to consider the perspective of the absent Bradys will prevent what happens from fully resolving the problem. In light of this fact, in order to resolve the conflict fully, the mediation panel needs to solicit a commitment from Ethel that she will *not* raise any further problem about use of the kitchen in the evening after the solution agreed upon by Bill and herself is implemented. This commitment may serve as the quid pro quo for Bill's willingness to purchase a new dishwasher or make other adjustments which may or may not be legally required.

Through the means summarized here, the mediation panel may guide the parties to a resolution of this conflict, without either party being subjected to the delays, costs, and uncertainty of litigation. The outcome is far preferable because both parties are able to walk away with a satisfactory result produced through far less investment. These benefits are quite critical for Bill, who could not have kept the Bradys on the line for the amount of time court proceedings would have consumed.

Situation No. 4
A Custody Dispute

A couple is in the midst of a divorce, ending a marriage of 12 years. They have two children, a son 10 years of age and a daughter 8 years of age. Under statutes requiring such in California, the couple began mediation of child custody and visitation issues.

For a time, it appeared that everything would be agreed upon with some effort. Both parents were amenable to joint legal custody and

APPLICATION TO VARIED SETTINGS 177

shared physical custody of the children. When discussion continued, however, concerning the precise periods of time that the children would spend with each parent, a significant dispute arose.

The parents are diametrically opposed concerning what religious upbringing the children should receive. The father is Jewish and the mother is a Protestant Christian. The father is adamant that the children should receive Jewish religious instruction, and should not be exposed to any Christian religious instruction. In order to assure that this occurs, he is insisting that he have physical custody of the children on all but a few weekends. The mother is insisting on precisely the opposite. She is adamant that the children should receive only Christian religious instruction, and she desires to have physical custody on most weekends in order to make certain that this takes place.

The Mediation Strategy

(1) Are All "Parties" at the Mediation Session?

(2) Working With a Manageable Number of Participants

This is a situation in which it is very likely that absent decision-makers are affecting the behavior of the parents. Where matters of religious upbringing are concerned, it can be expected that the grandparents may be influencing the views of the parents.

Thus far, this book has consistently advised that a mediator should take steps to assure that all absent decision-makers are involved in the mediation process. In this instance, the mediator's awareness that absent persons' views are possibly affecting the participants should not necessarily lead to inclusion of such absent persons in the process. If the grandparents are not actively involved in rearing of the children, their participation would probably broaden the mediation beyond a manageable scope and detract attention from the essential issues between the parents requiring attention.

Rather than including them, therefore, the mediator should make certain that each parent has thought about whether positions adopted simply espouse someone else's "party line," rather than reflecting the outcome the parent knows to be appropriate in light of the children's interests. Those interests must be given priority and brought into focus through the means described in the following sections.

Grandparents are not the only "absentees" likely to affect the parents in this dispute. If the parents have lawyers, they will also be influenced by the advice and actions of those lawyers. The mediator must take steps which maximize the chances for making this influence constructive rather than destructive. It should never be presumed that all lawyers will know what part they ought to play with reference to the mediation. The mediator should contact the lawyers to make sure they are familiar with the process. It will be highly important to remind them that if anyone makes "surprise moves," such as filing papers that ask for immediate court action, the angry reaction of the other side could destroy hard-won gains toward conciliation being accomplished in mediation. Lawyers should be asked to contact the mediator and confer about the status of the mediation before making any moves toward court.

If the cooperation of counsel is secured, they may be of help as the mediation progresses. Should a good solution be under discussion which one parent resists, despite the fact that all interests are appropriately protected, the mediator may discuss the status of the mediation with their lawyer. The lawyer may be encouraged to help the client recognize that this solution is preferable to any alternatives. Before any solution can be promoted, however, considerable work will be necessary, as suggested by the remaining sections below.

(9) *The Order of Attack*

(14) *Converting "Agreements in Theory" to Agreements in Fact*

The discussion of the earlier situations emphasizes that an initial joint session in which each party explains its point of view to the mediator generally causes both disputants to hear things they have never allowed themselves to hear before. While this is generally true, a mediator must always remain alert for circumstances indicating that particular animosity exists and that something must be done preliminarily to "unclog" the parties' ears before they will be able to listen constructively to anything. Divorce and resulting conflicts over parental roles or money frequently lead to such highly charged emotions.

For these reasons, mediators who work frequently with custody disputes customize the "order of attack" in a variety of ways to increase the likelihood that each party will really listen to the other's point of view. Some mediators begin by asking each parent to privately make a list of all the hopes or goals they have for their children. Invariably, when the lists are compared, two divorcing parents who thought themselves to be diametrically opposed find that they still have many common aspirations for their children. This recognition can help to enhance prospects for listening as each parent begins to explain their attitude about matters in dispute.

As discussions progress, the mediator may also use these areas of agreement as reference points (even "pressure points") when urging changes in position. More often than not, the parents will list goals that cannot possibly be achieved unless they reduce the animosity between themselves and cooperate toward maintaining healthy relationships among the children and each of the parents. The mediator can help the parties to convert their "agreements in theory" about hopes or goals for the children to agreements in fact.

Another approach sometimes used by mediators in this field is as follows: while one parent is explaining his or her perspective, the other parent is asked to turn around, facing away from the discussion, and pretend not to be there at all. It might seem that this would discourage listening, but it can have precisely the opposite effect. Someone who is told to pretend to be out of the room is highly unlikely to interrupt what is being said between the mediator and the other parent. Because the party cannot interrupt, but remains vitally interested in what is going on, he or she is inclined to listen much more intently. This tactic is really a specialized way to assure compliance with a policy against interruptions.

The "order of attack" can be adjusted in other ways to facilitate better listening. No single approach is mandatory. It is, however, necessary for successful mediation to customize the "order of attack" in light of the parties' particular circumstances.

(17) What Are Each Party's Pressures Points

In this case, both parents have a common concern that should motivate them to adopt more conciliatory positions. Both parents should share a paramount concern over the welfare of the children. Unfortunately, however, when there is hostility between divorcing parents, children are frequently made tools for the infliction of harm, since standing in the way of the other parent's wishes for the child is a ready means of inflicting considerable anguish. When this is true, the mediator must bring the common interest of the parents back into focus by reminding them that they both care about the emotional well-being of their children and that fighting over them or standing in the way of the other parent's relationship with a child can only be harmful.

The statute in California which requires mediation of child custody and visitation matters emphasizes the need to keep both parents focused upon a common concern for the children's welfare. California Code of Civil Procedure Section 4607(a) states:

> The purpose of such mediation proceedings shall be to reduce acrimony which may exist between the parties and to develop an agreement assuring the child or children *close and continuing contact with both parents* (emphasis added).

In the present circumstance, the mediator will need to spend considerable time with both parents making certain that they not only recognize a common concern for the welfare of the children, but, more importantly, recognize that the children's welfare will not be well served unless they have "a close and continuing" relationship with both parents. Here, it is certainly appropriate to counsel both parents that such a "close and continuing" relationship will not be possible if the religious tradition of either parent is completely suppressed.

It must be recognized, of course, that while this task may be easily stated, actually changing the parents' approaches will demand time and skill.

(12) *Pressing for Known Facts and Discovering Unknown Facts*

The discussion above concerning the pressure points that have relevance to this case should provide the means to make both parents more conciliatory, but it does not point toward any particular solution. Pressing for known facts and discovering unknown facts is the technique most likely to lead to a specific solution.

The children in this circumstance are not toddlers. The older child has been in school for five years, and the younger child has been in school for three years. The parents have, in all likelihood, been doing something about the children's religious instruction during the time prior to breakup of the marriage. Seemingly, each now wishes to deviate from past habits as a means to secure some victory related to the divorce.

The mediator should take steps to establish what the prior arrangement was concerning religious upbringing of the children. The children, at ages eight and ten, may also have some wishes in this area, and the mediator may attempt to discover them. This information should create movement toward a solution which is consistent with the family's habits before a divorce created reason to argue over the children.

A solution to this dispute forged by the parents themselves during mediation will create a resolution far superior to anything a court might do. The welfare of children will be adversely affected as long as there is hostility between their parents, and courts do not have the power to end hostility. A mediator, however, may help the parents to recognize that their own objectives for their children require them to work cooperatively on issues about upbringing.

Situation No. 5
A Family Problem

Mrs. Brooks is a single parent who works all day. She has had some difficulty controlling her son, Tom, who has missed a considerable amount of school. Recently, a school counselor sent Mrs. Brooks a letter informing her that the school was on the verge of taking action against Tom for truancy. The letter provided that Mrs. Brooks and Tom could use a special family mediation project, and that action alleging truancy would be withheld for a specified period of time to allow this.

The Mediation Strategy

(11) Peeling the Artichoke—Finding the Heart of the Matter

Mediation of this problem will best be served by beginning with a joint meeting of the sort described in Situation No. 3, The Neighborhood Problem. In that session, the mediator should pose certain questions to both Mrs. Brooks and Tom in order to make sure that everyone learns what is at the heart of the matter.

Tom should be pressed to explain why he has not attended school regularly. For purposes of discussion here, we will suppose that when pressed, Tom has several things to say. At the beginning of this school year, his mother informed him that he would be grounded one week for every day he missed from school. Under that penalty system, he quickly found himself in a position where he could not see daylight.

Once he had accumulated a month of grounded time, he saw no point in attending school regularly, since he could not look forward to evening activities any time in the foreseeable future anyway.

If this is Tom's response, then the mediator should ask Mrs. Brooks why she has imposed such a stringent penalty and whether she would be willing to adjust it in order to give Tom a clean start and some incentive to keep himself out of trouble. For purposes of discussion here, we may suppose that Mrs. Brooks will respond by explaining that she imposed a stringent penalty because she felt she was losing control of her son and that she would be hesitant to wipe the slate clean since she is not certain she can trust her son. In the past, the school counselor has sent notes to Mrs. Brooks through her son which were never delivered.

(15) Creativity—How Does the Mediator Promote New Ideas?

The events described above suggest a need for new ideas. Tom wants an opportunity for a clean start, but his mother is hesitant to give it to him because of his past conduct. Mother and son do not see a way out because they are only looking at the question of whether Tom attends school. They have not looked to any other aspect of their relationship in the hope of finding a key to the problem.

The mediator, however, may promote new ideas by directing them to other aspects of their relationship. Mrs. Brooks essentially wants to see some indication that Tom is ready for a clean start and that trust from her would not be misplaced. There must be other things necessary and helpful to the family that Tom could do in order to convince his mother that he is prepared to be more responsible. If Tom makes and fulfills a commitment to assume some added responsibility within the household this action should be sufficient to convince his mother that new-found trust is warranted.

The mediator may encourage the parties to explore these ideas. Such exploration could well lead to an agreement calling for: (1) Assumption of added household responsibility by Tom to establish that he is ready for a second chance, followed by; (2) Withdrawal of current grounding penalties; and (3) An agreed upon system of penalties for any additional absences from school.

The Children's Hearing Project of the Massachusetts Advocacy Center has published several case histories representing successful mediations it has conducted concerning family problems. One, which it describes as Case Study Number 2, has characteristics similar to this situation. The Children's Hearing Project was able to bring the parties to agreement within a two-hour session, and, after three months, the son had not missed any school whatsoever.

The use of mediation to address this problem clearly accomplished much more than pursuing the son as a truant could have. Mediation rebuilt the relationship between this mother and son in a way that can be expected to have a positive impact on many dimensions of their lives.

Chapter 4

Comparing Mediation to the Alternatives

Before mediation may be compared to near and distant cousins, an inventory of the alternatives must be presented. Throughout human history, people have used a variety of means to end their conflicts. These means, however, fall into a limited number of categories. The categories are defined below, with the benefits and detriments common to each noted.

Force

The age-old way to settle differences is through force— the survival of the most fit. If the controversy is one between schoolboys, that may mean a fist fight. Needless to say, this "technique" is not limited to schoolboys. If the controversy is between management and labor, the force used is economic power. The union may strike or management may resort to lockout. The side which can survive economically the longest comes out on top. If the controversy is between nations, force may take several different forms. A country may impose trade quotas or withhold aid because it hopes to force action by some foreign government. In the worst case, of course, the use of force by countries means war.

The benefits and detriments of this device are clear. The "most fit" expect this method to be a successful means for imposing their will. Some harm, however, is always experienced by both parties, and sometimes the injuries to the winner are just as great as those suffered by the loser.

Negotiation

Negotiation is the best technique for the settlement of disputes, because any agreement reached is the joint product of the parties.

By negotiation, the parties themselves, without the intervention of outsiders, seek to persuade each other to an agreement over whatever matters are in dispute. How do they do this? Sometimes pure reason prevails, but more often than not, the participants make progress by reminding each other of the alternatives to agreement—which generally include some kind of force, be it a strike, a war, or a consumer boycott. If negotiations break down, participants may resort to force, which highlights the weakness of this method. There is no certainty of success. Participants must make use of one of the other alternatives in this inventory if negotiations fail.

Sometimes various structures are added to the negotiation process in the thought that they will improve chances for success. Parties who must regularly negotiate with one another sometimes agree to perform *joint fact finding* before addressing settlement proposals. This process is an effort by representatives of each party to agree jointly on as many relevant facts as possible. Joint fact finding can aid decision makers because they have a clearer idea of what has led to a dispute when they consider the merits of possible settlements.

Some statutes controlling the labor relations of employees who work in government jobs call for a different kind of *fact finding*. Under such statutes, when negotiations fail, the parties are required to call in a neutral fact finder who accumulates facts relevant to the disputed matters and summarizes them in a report. The hope is that such a report will motivate changes in the parties' positions. If that hope is not realized, however, the parties must resort to some other method to reach agreement.

If the parties either agree or acquiesce, the fact finder(s) may take a more active role by employing mediation techniques such as those discussed in this book. Without such intervention, prospects that a fact-finding report will induce settlement of and by itself are remote.

Mediation

Mediation occurs when one or more people who have no direct stake in a dispute participate in negotiations between the disputants for the purpose of assisting the parties to reach a settlement. One critical thing must be noted about mediation. A mediator does not have the power to impose any outcome on the parties. Since mediation is a continuation of the negotiation process, it will not produce a resolution unless everyone affected agrees to it. The comparative benefits of mediation are discussed at the conclusion of this chapter.

A word should be said here about the term *conciliation*. Some people use this word interchangeably with mediation. Others draw a distinction, but there is unfortunately no uniformity to the distinctions various people make. In the United States, most authors who distinguish between the two terms use the word conciliation to describe a process in which the neutral participant(s) employ a range of devices to improve communication and prospects for settlement between the parties, but *refrain* from making any concrete proposals about settlement.

The term mediation is reserved for circumstances in which the neutral participant works actively as a third negotiator, advocating concrete suggestions for settlement, as displayed in this book. In Europe, however, the term conciliation is frequently used to describe this more active form of involvement by neutral participants. It is important, therefore, for persons involved in international disputes to make certain that the intended meaning of terms chosen is made clear.

Arbitration

Parties to a dispute can, having failed in negotiation and/or mediation, agree to submit the issues in dispute to an outsider playing a different role than that of a mediator, i.e., an arbitrator. The parties give an arbitrator the authority to render final and binding decisions about all matters in dispute. This authority is given before presenting any information to the arbitrator about the problems. Such decisions may be converted into a court judgment, and in most instances the court will not reexamine the merits of the case presented in arbitration. Clearly, an arbitrator serves a much different role than a mediator. An arbitrator acts like a private judge and decides what the solution will be. By contrast, a mediator can only encourage agreement upon a solution.

In comparison to mediation, arbitration offers the benefit of certainty that an end will be declared to the dispute. In order to accomplish this, however, the parties must turn resolution of their problem over to someone else.

The arbitration process can be adapted in a number of ways. Some parties agree that both disputants will submit their "final offer" on a disputed matter to an arbitrator who will be asked to declare one or the other of the offers to be the outcome. The arbitrator has no discretion to impose a compromise solution. The theory behind this *final offer* system is that both parties will be motivated to put forth reasonable final offers, thereby enhancing prospects for settlement without any need to call in an outsider.

It creates confusion when this process is called "arbitration" because that word has historically described the rendition of a binding decision found appropriate on the basis of record evidence submitted by the parties. Because an "arbitrator" under a "final offer" system is given no discretion, he or she may end up imposing an outcome without being at all convinced that such outcome is warranted by the record evidence—it is simply declared to be the lesser of two evils.

In many court systems, some parties are required to submit their cases to a form of nonbinding arbitration. The courts cannot require binding arbitration where there is no agreement to use it because this would force people to forgo rights protected by the federal and state Constitutions, such as the right to a jury trial. To help relieve court congestion, therefore, *nonbinding* arbitration is used. The hope is that many litigants will feel they have had "their day in court" and will accept the result after it is declared by the arbitrator(s), even though there is no requirement that they do so.

Frequently, the system increases chances for such acceptance by providing that parties who go on to court and fail to do better there are made liable for costs of the other party, which they would not otherwise have had to pay. There is some coercion to accept the arbitration result, therefore.

This is another somewhat confusing development. In the past, arbitration has had two central traits: it has been voluntary and binding. *Court-annexed arbitration* is missing the two positive attributes which have made arbitration beneficial in the past. It looks somewhat like fat-free, salt-free bacon—robbed of everything that made it good!

Because many "arbitrators" working under such systems want to improve the chance that their participation will bring a satisfactory conclusion to the dispute, they sometimes take it upon themselves to act as mediators. This fact is causing many people to be unclear about the differences between mediation and arbitration. Acceptance for both processes is enhanced when the professionals in charge take the time to explain carefully the differences and make sure that all parties are prepared to use a particular process before it is undertaken. Thus, the prospect that any participant's expectations will not be met is reduced and participants achieve a greater understanding of what role they need to play.

Mediation-Arbitration (Med-Arb)

This process combines the informality of mediation with the finality of arbitration. Parties using this process agree that the med-arbiter has the authority to make a final and binding decision on the issues in dispute. However, the med-arbiter is asked first to exhaust all efforts at settlement through mediation. Thus, as many questions as possible are solved through voluntary agreement. All solutions, both those agreed upon and those resolved by the med-arbiter, are included in the med-arbiter's final, enforceable decision. This process maximizes the opportunity for the parties to reach mutually acceptable solutions to matters in dispute, while still assuring final and binding resolutions that may prevent any resort to force.

Some parties have combined mediation with nonbinding arbitration to create *Med-Rec*, i.e., mediation followed by a recommendation. At first blush, it may seem pointless to follow mediation with a nonbinding recommendation. In disputes where the parties are subject to political pressures, however, the recommendation may have significant impact.

Courts

In all fields of law, it is ideal if parties first use negotiation to settle disputes. If this technique fails to bring about a settlement, one or the other party may sometimes resort to litigation. Unlike the processes discussed above, courts are *not* available to solve all sorts of problems. Historically, our courts have only been available to settle disputes about *existing* rights. Two parties may not walk into court and say, "We want to have a contract, but we cannot agree on any of its terms. Please decide on what they should be." The court will *not* write an entire contract for the parties establishing their future rights. If future rights are not of enough importance to warrant legislation, the parties must work them out through negotiation, mediation, arbitration, med-arb, and/or force, all of which can be used for this purpose.

Court procedures and arbitration have certain features in common. Both in court and in arbitration, the parties present facts through witnesses and arguments. Then, someone else (a jury, judge, or arbitrator) decides the outcome. There are, however, significant differences between court trials and arbitration. Court trials are quite formal. Because courts are a branch of the government, they must follow many rules and procedures that are designed to protect the participants from unfair government action.

When parties arbitrate, they try to select an arbitrator with background and experience regarding their type of problem. This selection gives them confidence that their case will be understood and properly decided *without* the formality, rules, and procedures of a court trial. In essence, the parties trade in the formalism and rules of court for the expertise of a decision maker (an arbitrator) in whom they have confidence. As a result of this trade, arbitration is generally less time-consuming and costly than court litigation.

Other Combinations of These Techniques

Parties can and often do use more than one of the techniques described thus far. For example, in the labor relations field, the parties will always start with direct negotiations and may then use mediation. If mediation fails, they may either agree to arbitrate or resort to strikes and lockouts.

As noted in the Introduction, legislation in some states requires parents who disagree over child custody or visitation rights to use mediators. Court commissioners frequently serve in this role. If this effort fails, the matter is then referred to the courts for a final decision. Many courts now have procedures that mandate efforts to settle other cases before trial. Sometimes these efforts are assisted by a judge or an experienced attorney who acts as a mediator.

The descriptions above make clear that parties have also created hybrid systems which simultaneously use more than one of the traditional methods to resolve disputes. Through creativity and flexibility the parties are able to mold the process to their needs. The range of acceptable methods for designing dispute-resolution systems is virtually limitless. Parties should feel free to fashion new approaches to meet their needs. However, care must be taken to assure that everyone has a similar understanding of the nature of the process being used. If they do not, conflicting expectations may lead to problems.

One new process combining parts of the above-described methods that has been found particularly useful by business organizations is called a *minitrial*. Variations exist in this process, but it typically has the following features. A neutral "advisor," generally an experienced attorney or judge, conducts an informal, private, and confidential hearing or meeting at which all sides present facts and argument regarding a dispute. To ensure that presentations remain focused and relevant, time limits are imposed on each party. A senior executive with the authority to settle the dispute attends on behalf of each party and listens to the presentations. After all summaries have been presented, the executives meet with the advisor and try to reach a settlement based upon what they have heard. If they are unsuccessful, the advisor may give an opinion about the likely outcome in court and/or a recommendation for settlement, depending upon the ground rules worked out in advance.

The conference of the senior executives with the advisor combines negotiation with mediation and might be called *Neg-Med*. Both negotiation and mediation are effective, in part, because *everyone* has heard a common presentation of the relevant facts and arguments. Before such a process, senior executives may be hearing an overly optimistic view of the case from attorneys or direct participants who have become wedded to a particular position. After jointly hearing the facts and arguments presented at the minitrial, each executive can more realistically evaluate strengths and weaknesses in the contentions. Thus, a negotiated settlement becomes more likely. And the advisor's evaluation carries added weight because everyone has heard the information upon which that evaluation is based.

Although a special name has been given to this process, the role played by the advisor is really quite similar to that played by most mediators. As displayed in earlier portions of this book, most mediations use joint meetings to assure that everyone is aware of the factual contentions and arguments of the parties. In addition, all mediators remind the parties of what will likely occur without an agreement. Labor mediators frequently question whether a given position is important enough to hold up an agreement, thereby leaving open the prospect of strike or lockout. Family Court Commissioners remind the parties of the results that can be expected if a matter is decided in court. The minitrial advisor is acting similarly when he or she forecasts how a case will be decided in court.

Is Mediation the Best of These?

It is clear from the foregoing that mediation is only one technique available to settle disputes. It is reasonable to ask, "Should mediation be a preferred technique, and, if so, why?"

There is absolutely no question that negotiation is the best way to solve problems. By definition, a negotiated solution is a solution satisfactory to all concerned, because it is made by the parties themselves and its acceptance is voluntary.

The simple fact of the matter is, however, that unassisted negotiation does not always succeed. When it does not, the next most desirable process is mediation because it brings with it all of the same benefits offered by negotiation. Any resolution of the dispute must be satisfactory to all concerned. This highlights a critical benefit mediation has when compared to litigation. No matter how strongly the law seems to support one party's position, the outcome in court is not a certainty. Litigation is a risky business. The law may change or the jury may see the facts differently than was forecast. Those who opt for mediation are not stuck with "a pig in a poke." They may establish the solution for their dispute with certainty. Even if it entails some sacrifice, that may be preferable to the risk of a court imposing greater sacrifice.

This emphasizes what is good about mediation when it works—it produces a solution that is agreeable to everyone. It must be acknowledged, of course, that even the most effective mediator sometimes cannot bring the parties to agreement. This has to be noted when comparing mediation to other techniques for resolving disputes. Arbitration, med-arb, and litigation all assure that some final solution will be imposed.

Even though mediation may not always produce a solution, it offers critical benefits over other settlement techniques that make it worth pursuing. As the examples in this book demonstrate, mediation is a creative process. One of the central things mediators accomplish is helping parties define their problems more precisely. Frequently, this better understanding of the problems at issue produces new proposed solutions. And these new proposed solutions may well be more palatable than anything previously discussed, thereby giving rise to a mutually acceptable settlement. Even when a full settlement cannot be attained, these positive features of mediation nearly always help to narrow the issues in dispute.

Such creative problem-solving is actually discouraged by litigation, rather than encouraged. Litigation necessarily entails the adoption of firm positions. The more fixed these positions become, the harder it is to identify the underlying problems that must be addressed to settle the differences between the parties. And there is a natural human tendency to stand firm on positions once taken in order to avoid any appearance that initial actions were ill conceived. Because mediation is a far more flexible process, parties may alter their postures without "losing face." Mediation does not declare a winner and a loser; it strives to declare all parties winners.

Thus, the aftermath of a successful mediation is generally cordial, since everyone has been made a winner. Unlike a court case, there are fewer causes for animosity between the parties. This feature of mediation is particularly important if the parties either *must* have or desire to have ongoing dealings, as is frequently true in labor, business, or family disputes. Situation No. 4 and Situation No. 5 from Chapter 3 demonstrate how valuable mediation can be in these circumstances.

There is a further benefit to mediation which makes it worth the investment of time even though an outcome may not be guaranteed. Some other alternatives can offer the surety of a solution, although it must be an imposed solution. There is no system, however, that can offer the assurance that this solution will be fully effectuated by any particular time. If a matter is litigated, the losing party may contest the result and appeals may go on for years. Parties may even contest the result of arbitration through litigation on some limited grounds. These features mean that a party may well spend more time trying to secure compliance with a judgment or award than it took to receive the judgment or award in the first place.

When mediation succeeds, it avoids this difficulty. Parties will typically comply with a settlement that they have voluntarily worked out together through mediation. Only in the rarest of circumstances will something preclude such compliance. It is worth investing time in mediation in order to strive for this central benefit. In short, mediation as displayed in this text has multiple virtues that make it one of the best "peacemaking" alternatives when direct negotiations fail.

Appendix

The following tables will be useful to you if you wish to track or recall positions advanced by the parties on economic issues during the course of the mediation.

Table A. Pension Benefits

Positions of the Parties Before Mediation

Management

    Continuation of Medical Insurance for Retirees

    Continuation of Instrument Insurance for Retirees

    2 tickets to each dress rehearsal

Union

    Guaranteed Payments:

1st Year	$15,000/year
2nd Year	$21,250/year
3rd Year	$28,500/year

Continuation of *all* fringe benefits (including eye care and dental, proposed for this agreement).

Positions in Mediation

Management [Day 3; 10:00 A.M.]	*Management* [Day 3; 4:30 P.M.]

1) Supplementary Pay:
   a) Age 70/30 years;
   b) *50%* weekly salary in last year times years up to 40;
   c) 2 payments per contract year
	1) Supplementary Pay:
	
	   b) *50%* weekly salary times years up to *45*
	
	   c) OK
	
	2) And,
	   a) OK (Med. Ins.)
	   b) OK (Instr. Ins.)
	   c) OK (Tickets)
	   d) No
	   e) Concept OK, if *not* voting
	3) Reg. Pension Rate: 7½% (current) ⟨on total earnings⟩

Union [Day 3; 3:30 P.M.]	*Union* [Day 3; 5:00 P.M.]

1) Supplementary Pay:
   a) OK
   b) *100%* weekly salary in last year times years up to 40;
   c) OK if cumulative
2) And,
   a) Med. Ins. for Musician & Spouse
   b) Instrument Ins.
   c) 2 Dress Rehearsal Tickets
   d) Dental Ins.
   e) Retirees stay in Barg. Unit
3) Reg. Pension Rate: 8½% on *total* earnings
	1) Supplementary Pay:
	   a) *75%* weekly salary times years up to *40*;
	
	2) And,
	
	   d) Dropped (Dental)
	   e) Retirees will not vote
	
	3) Reg. Pension Rate: 7½%/8%/8½% on *total* earnings

Positions in Mediation

Management [Day 3; 5:30 P.M.] 1) Supplementary Pay 　b) 50% weekly salary times years up to 45; 2) And, 　e) OK, but need language 3) Reg. Pension Rate: 7%/7½%/8%/8½% on *total* earnings	*Management* Prior Union Position Accepted. Issue Resolved.
Union [Day 3; 6:00 P.M.] 1) Supplementary Pay 　b) 60% weekly salary times years up to 38 2) And, 　e) Retiree issues negotiable 3) Reg. Pension Rate: 7%/7½%/8%/8½% on *total* earnings	

Table B. Time and Money Guarantees

Positions of the Parties Before Mediation

Management

    Continue *time guarantees* from expired agreement:
        20 Performance weeks
        12 Preliminary days
        80 Rehearsal hours

Union

    Weekly base rates of:

1st Year	$965
2nd Year	$1060
3rd Year	$1165

    Guaranteed annual income of:

1st Year	$30,000
2nd Year	$34,000
3rd Year	$38,000

Positions in Mediation

Management [Day 3; 8:30 P.M.]	*Management* [Day 4; 2:30 P.M.]
1) Guaranteed Time: Per expired agreement	1) Guaranteed Time: No change
2) Money: No new position	2) Money: Base rates for 4 years $785/$825/$865/$905
3) Supplemental Pay: a) $ = ? b) All Opera-generated income counts; & c) Work turned down causes reduction	
Union [Day 4; 10:00 A.M.]	*Union* [Day 4; 3:10 P.M.]
For Year #1 - 1) Guaranteed Time: a) 20 Performance weeks; b) 15 Preliminary days; c) 100 Rehearsal hours; & d) 15 Days for ballet 2) Money: a) Base rate = $815 b) 3 weeks vacation c) 1 week minimum seniority pay 3) Supplemental Pay: Expected earnings = $29,500	2) Money: Year 1 Base rate $965

Positions in Mediation

Management
[Day 4; 3:30 P.M.]
 	
2) Money:
   Base rates for 4 years
   $795/$835/$875/$915
	Management
	[Day 6; 3:00 P.M.]
	
	2) Money:
	   Base rates for 4 years
	   $800/$835/$875/$915
	3) Supplemental pay:
	   $1500/$1600/$1700/$1800

Union
[Day 6; 11:30 A.M.]
For Year #1 -
 	
2) Money:
   a) Base rate = $810
   b) Dropped ("vacation")
   c) 2 week minimum seniority pay
	Union
	[Day 6; 4:50 P.M.]
	
	2) Money:
	   a) Base rates for 3 Years
	   $800/$900/$1000
	
	3) Supplemental pay:
	   $1750/$2250/$2750

Positions in Mediation

Management [Day 6; 7:10 P.M.]	*Management* [Day 7; 12:10 A.M.]
2) Money: Base rates for 4 years $800/$845/$885/$925 3) Supplemental Pay: $1600/$1600/$1700/$1800	2) Money: Base rates for 3 years $800/$850/$900 3) Supplemental Pay: $1600/$1700/$1800
Union [Day 6; 9:10 P.M.]	*Union* [Day 7; 1:10 A.M.]
2) Money: Base rates for 3 years $800/$895/$985 3) Supplemental Pay: $1600/$2250/$2750	2) Money: Base rates for 3 years $800/$885/$975 3) Supplemental Pay: $1600/$2000/$2500

Positions in Mediation

Management [Day 10; 5:00 P.M.]	*Management* [Day 10; 7:45 P.M.]

1) Guaranteed Time:
   a) 20 Performance weeks
   b) 12 Preliminary days
   c) 85 Rehearsal hours
2) Money:
   a) Base rates for 3 years $800/$860/$920
   b&c) Existing seniority pay with 2 week min. tenured & 1 week min. nontenured
3) Supplemental pay:
   a) Annual guarantee for tenured & nontenured =
   T- $25,000/$27,000/$30,000
   NT- $23,000/$25,000/$27,000
   b) All Opera-generated income counts; &
   c) Work turned down causes reduction
	Everything Accepted

Union [Day 10; 7:30 P.M.]	
Everything Accepted IF increase to 8½% for regular pension contributions moved to 3rd year of agreement.	

Index

A

Agreement (*see* Settlement agreement)
Arbitration 107
   alternative to mediation 11, 16, 91, 154
   litigation compared 188–189
   med-arb 11, 16, 188
   precedential value of prior award 87–89, 129–130
   process described 186–187
Arbitrator's role 19–20, 139, 187

B

Blinders problem 124, 126, 133
Brown v. Board of Education 149
Business disputes 4, 107, 137, 158–163

C

California 176, 180
Child custody disputes 106, 138, 176–181, 189
Civil disputes 107
Civil suits (*see* Litigation)
Collective bargaining agreements
   enforcement 106–107, 156
   mediator's review 20–21, 90, 94, 127
Commercial disputes 137, 158–163
Conciliation 186
Confidence (*see* Trust)
Confidentiality, of private meetings 18, 54–56
Conflict identification
   determining heart of matter 2, 12–13, 43–44, 61–62, 67, 123–125, 174–175, 181–182
   exposing specific problems 64–66, 89–92, 94–95
   facts identification 2, 25, 33, 98, 125–129, 160–161, 164, 166–168
   parties' views 2, 9, 11–12, 15–16, 85–88, 93, 123, 159–160, 162
   review of prior contracts 20–21, 90

Conflict resolution strategies
   avoid errors in transmission 30–31, 37, 53
   clarify proposals 2, 27–28, 35–37, 40–49, 62–64, 68–70, 77–78, 97–99
   discourage outrageous positions 33, 60, 78, 100
   encourage flexibility 10, 66
   explain consequences of positions taken 88–89, 130–131
   explore options 13, 67–68, 101–103
   follow up on success 52–53, 85–86, 96
   generate new ideas 2, 25, 43, 44, 90–94, 132–135, 182–183
   horsetrading 2, 37–40, 135–136
   identify parties' most important goals 72, 81, 96–97, 99–100, 143
   mediator's control of 31, 53
   order of discussion 2, 39–40, 66, 73, 81–82, 85–86, 120–123, 159, 165–166, 178–179
   parties' intention to avoid future conflict 39
   pocket concessions 41–42, 146–148
   push for progress on specifics 2, 13–15, 21–24, 29–30, 45–46, 53–54, 66, 73–80, 82, 95–97, 104–105
   realistic optimism 1, 10–11, 17, 31–32, 61, 81, 85, 116–117
   suggest specific language 2, 46, 54, 56–58, 154–155
   uncover possible movement 77, 96
Conversion of issues 124–125
Courts (*see also* Litigation)
   dispute settlement role 188–189
   involvement in arbitration 187
Creativity requirement 2, 25, 43, 44, 90–94, 132–135, 182–183

D

Discovery (*see also* Facts) 163
Drafting of agreement (*see* Settlement agreement)

E

Employer committees 7
Enforcement 2, 106–107, 156–157
Environmental disputes 111

F

Facilitators 6–7
Fact finding 185
Facts
  identification 2, 25, 33, 98, 125–129, 160–161, 164, 166–168
  interpretation and use 71–72, 105, 129–131, 180–181
Fairness concerns 59–60, 139–140
  discourage dickering 78, 100
  discourage outrageous positions 33, 60
Family disputes
  child custody 106, 176–181, 189
  child truancy 181–183
  pressure points 4–5, 138
Forceful conflict resolution 184

G

Grayrocks Dam project 111

H

Horsetrading 2, 37–39, 135–136

I

Issue identification (*see* Conflict identification)

J

Joint fact finding 185
Joint meetings
  decision-makers' presence at 1, 7–8, 50–51, 54, 110–111, 161–162, 173
  location 2, 119
  manageable number of participants 1, 5–6, 112–113, 177–178
  purpose and agenda 8, 16–17, 24–25, 84, 114–116, 162, 165–166, 173–174, 178

L

Labor relations 189
Language suggestions 2, 46, 54, 56–58, 154–155
Legal advice 49–52

Listening requirement
  hearing other party's views 24, 114–115, 162, 165–166, 174, 178–179
  mediator, listening before persuading 19, 113, 151, 175
Litigation
  arbitration compared 188–189
  mediation alternative 149–151
  threat of, as "pressure point" 4–5, 137, 148, 170
Location of meetings 2, 119
Lockout threat 4, 184, 189

M

Med-arb 11, 16, 188
Media bans 9–10, 16, 17
Mediation
  alternatives to 2, 11, 16, 153–154, 184–190
  conciliation compared 186
  as negotiating tool 6, 185–186, 190–192
  preparatory agreement 18
Mediation agreement (*see* Settlement agreement)
Mediation strategies (*see* Conflict resolution strategies)
Mediator's role
  acquainting parties with process 18
  arbitrator distinguished 19–20, 139
  becoming acquainted with parties 1, 8, 113–114
  developing parties' trust 2, 9, 61, 106, 118–119, 138, 152–153, 166, 167
  drafting language 2, 46, 54, 56–58, 154–155
  listening before persuading 19, 113, 151, 175
  overview 109
  realistic optimism 1, 10–11, 17, 81, 85, 116–117
  third negotiator 2, 6–7, 19, 20, 53–54, 58–60, 76–77, 96–97, 100, 139–151, 169–172, 175
  useful character traits 107–108, 157
Meetings (*see* Joint meetings; Private meetings)
Minitrials 163, 189–190
Money and time guarantees 196–200

N

National Aeronautics and Space Administration (NASA) 158, 163
Nebraska 111

Neg-med   190
Negotiation   184–185, 189–191
Negotiation committees   7
Neighborhood disputes   172–176
Note-taking accuracy   30–31, 37, 53

O

Optimism   1, 10–11, 17, 31–32, 61, 81, 85, 116–117
Order of discussion   2, 39–40, 66, 73, 81–82, 85–86, 120–123, 159, 165–166, 178–179

P

Parties
  decision-makers' presence at meeting   1, 7–8, 50–51, 54, 110–111, 161–162, 173
  identification of non-participants   9
  individual priorities   2, 9, 11–12, 123, 159–160, 162
  manageable number   1, 5–6, 112–113, 177–178
  mediator's becoming acquainted with   1, 8, 113–114
  trust   2, 9, 61, 106, 118–119, 138, 152–153, 166, 167
Patience requirement   2, 19, 24, 73, 106, 117–118
Pension benefits   193–195
Persuaders   6–7
Pocket concessions   41–42, 146–148
Pressure points
  concept defined   2, 4, 136–137
  utilization of   4–5, 18–19, 60, 137–138, 149–150, 161, 163, 170, 179–180
Private meetings
  confidentiality   18, 54–56
  location   2, 119
  propriety and usefulness   5, 8, 11–12, 16, 17, 21–22, 26, 53, 84–85, 115–116, 123, 130, 166–168
Public opinion   5

R

Ratification of agreement   8

S

"Secret hearts" of parties   2, 53, 112, 138–139, 144, 168–169
Settlement agreement
  confirmation of tentative agreements   2, 48, 131–132, 176, 178–179
  enforcement   2, 106–107, 156–157
  prompt drafting   2, 48, 54, 103–104, 132, 155
  ratification   8
  suggesting specific language   2, 46, 54, 56–58, 154–155
Sexual harassment disputes   163–172
Shuttle diplomacy   1, 24, 26, 53, 84, 114–116, 165–166
Signals from parties   26–27, 151, 152
Simkin, William   107–108
SpaceCom Corp.,   163
Strategies (*see* Conflict resolution strategies)
Strike threat   4, 137, 184, 189
Susskind, Lawrence   111

T

Talking (*see* Listening requirement)
Tentative agreement (*see* Settlement agreement)
Time and money guarantees   196–200
Timing concerns (*see also* Pressure points)
  overview   2, 152–153, 162–164, 175
  presentation of proposals   21–22, 75, 77, 83, 96, 106
  signals from parties   26–27, 151, 152, 162
Trust
  in mediation process   61, 152–153
  in mediator   2, 9, 106, 118–119, 138, 166, 167
TRW, Inc.,   163

U

Union representatives   7

W

Wyoming   111

About the Authors

Sam Kagel has been since 1945 and is currently active full time as an arbitrator and mediator in labor and commercial cases, as well as all other types of employment disputes. He was Professor of Law for 16 years at Boalt Hall School of Law, University of California at Berkeley, where he taught courses in arbitration, mediation, negotiation, and labor law. His second edition of *The Anatomy of a Labor Arbitration* was published by the Bureau of National Affairs, Inc., in 1986. He is a founding member of the Royal Academy of Arbitrators.

Kathy Kelly is Professor of Law at McGeorge School of Law, University of the Pacific, Sacramento, California, where she teaches negotiation skills, arbitration practice, alternative dispute resolution, and civil procedure. She has served and continues to serve as mediator, Special Master, or arbitrator in all types of employment disputes and many other kinds of lawsuits. Her writings include "Labor Arbitration: Cutting Cost and Time Without Cutting Quality," in the September 1985 issue of the *Arbitration Journal*, and the chapter on "Some Legal Aspects of Arbitration" in *The Anatomy of a Labor Arbitration*. She also is a member of the Royal Academy of Arbitrators.